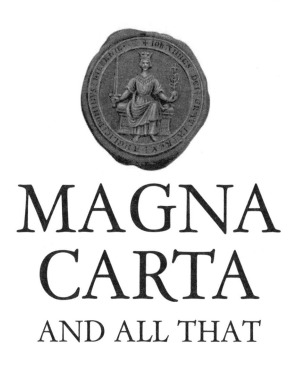

MAGNA
CARTA
AND ALL THAT

A guide to the Magna Carta
and life in England in 1215

ANDRE
DEUTSCH

THIS IS AN ANDRÉ DEUTSCH BOOK

Published in 2015 by André Deutsch Limited
A division of the Carlton Publishing Group
20 Mortimer Street
London W1T 3JW

10 9 8 7 6 5 4 3 2 1

Text and design copyright © André Deutsch Limited 2015

A catalogue record for this book is available from the British Library

ISBN 978 0 233 00464 8

Printed and bound by CPI Group (UK) Ltd, Croydon, CR0 4YY

CONTENTS

Contents

KEY TO SYMBOLS

Each entry is categorised into one of four main themes running throughout the book. These are marked by the following symbols:

 = the Charter itself

 = Key people involved in the making of Magna Carta

 = Medieval society

 = Places of importance

INTRODUCTION

Over the past 800 years, Magna Carta has been invoked by politicians, lawyers and statesmen throughout the English-speaking world to add drama and gravitas to their own speeches and declarations. The medieval document is cited as a triumph of liberty and justice, but it really wasn't that at all.

Magna Carta has been hailed as the document that established the legal rights of the people of England, endowing all of England's inhabitants with legal protection from exploitation and establishing the concept that everyone was equal in the eyes of the law. It really wasn't that, either.

Magna Carta was even cited by United States congressman Peter Rodino, who, as Chairman of the House Judiciary Committee, oversaw the impeachment proceedings that were initiated against President Richard Nixon in 1974. Rodino described how the English barons had forced King John to agree to the wording of the Great Charter "at the point of a sword", the congressman's point being that the document established the idea that no man, not even a king, should be able to hold himself above the law. Magna Carta did do that, although English kings, including John, would attempt to conveniently overlook this concept whenever it suited them. After the original charter was issued in 1215, however, they did so at their peril.

When the charter was first issued, it simply served to plunge England into yet another war. However, Magna Carta could not be trampled upon by a king's cavalry or lost in the smoke of battle. Once the document existed, it took on a life of its own, changing, developing and growing in stature. Where clauses were found to be unworkable or other changes and additions needed making, there were always lawyers and statesmen ready to push the changes through and maintain the rule of law rather than risk returning to the absolute rule of a monarch.

As such, Magna Carta was reissued in 1216, 1217, 1225 and 1297, with further revisions appearing throughout the subsequent turbulent centuries of England's history.

Not everyone who came into power had a great deal of respect for the charter. Oliver Cromwell, who ruled as Lord Protector of the Commonwealth of England, Scotland and Ireland from 1653 until his death (from natural causes) in 1658, famously (and rudely) dismissed the charter as "Magna Farta" when it was cited in debate. Cromwell was peacefully buried in Westminster Abbey until the royalists returned to power and had his body exhumed so that he could be posthumously beheaded. Whether that served as a warning to others not to disrespect the charter however, the agreement certainly came to be regarded as the foundation stone of government in England. Yet, that really wasn't what it was originally intended for either.

In reality, the charter was about wealth and power. What the barons wanted to do was to maintain their own families' riches and influence by forcing the king to agree to their demands. They would not have had any inkling, and would not have cared much, that the steps they were taking would later enshrine a legal document as an icon of democracy.

In order to understand the barons' motives, and even to understand the document itself, it is helpful to know a bit about England in 1215 and how society was organized at that time. To do that, we'll need to get to know some of the characters and families involved. There are, therefore, a number of short biographies scattered throughout the book, identifying some of the "Major Players". These, of course, include King John and his troublesome barons, but also a number of women who might not at first seem to have much of a connection with Magna Carta. Chief amongst them is Eleanor of Aquitaine.

Why Eleanor? She was, of course, King John's mother, but she died more than 11 years before the events at Runnymede and made no direct contribution to negotiating the terms of the charter agreement. She merits a more extensive mention than most because her family history and her life story prove a revealing illustration of how agreements during the medieval period could be struck and then abandoned in the blink of an eye. The way Eleanor protected her family's interests surely demonstrated to John the insidious and scheming double-dealing and backsliding that was key to keeping your hands on the reins of power.

As mother to the Plantagenet brothers (Henry the Young King, King Richard I, Geoffrey and King John), Eleanor played her sons against each other in struggles over power and territory. She sided with her boys when they fought against Henry II, her husband and their father. "Plantagenet" was Henry II's family name, actually a nickname given to his father and thought to be based on his use of the common broom plant – *planta genista* in Latin – as his emblem. Despite having married into the Plantagenet family, Eleanor's aim was always to hold on to any land and property that she saw as hers. She even joined forces with her former husband, King Louis VII of France, to try to remove Henry from the throne of England when she thought that he might do something silly – such as bequeath land and titles to one of his illegitimate children instead of leaving everything to her family. Maintaining the wealth and power that stemmed from the territory that her family controlled was certainly what motivated Eleanor, and, as with all other wealthy aristocrats, she passed on to her children the notion of fighting for what you believed to be yours.

"Fighting" in the twelfth and thirteenth centuries was not generally a euphemism for boardroom or courtroom battles, where words, writs, law suits and legal documents were the chosen weapons – although those did exist. Fighting, however, usually meant violent clashes. These were brutal times and any kind of confrontation, from a border dispute to a pitched battle was a hideously grisly affair played out as close-quarter combat. Firearms were not widely known in Europe until the fourteenth century, so archers were the artillery of the day, although the trebuchet "catapult" and other siege engines were used to break down castle walls. Fighting was thus done hand-to-hand, with knights, who would become barons, learning how to kill with the lance, the sword, the axe, the hammer and all manner of sinister weaponry. Fighting meant facing the enemy only an arm's length away – bodies were split open and limbs lopped off at close enough range for the victors to become drenched in the blood of the vanquished. For men used to settling scores in this way, resorting to "fighting" the king with a mere document was something of a novelty.

Magna Carta is one among many documents issued by King John, and the major landowners also issued charters from their own courts to cover the grant of land or to settle disputes. The Great Charter was so called simply because it was more extensive than any other, and dared to go so far as to limit the power of the king.

Their aim, of course, was to try to curb the excessive financial demands of the king without there being yet another war. Wars were an expensive business and recovering from a major conflict, leaving aside the lives lost and people maimed, could take years. This book will take a closer look at what motivated the barons and why exactly they wanted to avoid a costly war.

To help put Magna Carta further in context, and to show how it was intended to change the lives of some of the population – while leaving others with little or no benefit – the book will examine the way people lived, from the ordinary peasants to the great lords and ladies. It will describe their homes, and the kinds of work they did in order to feed their families and keep a roof over their heads – whether they were aristocrats or lowly field hands. We will find out how people dressed and what they ate, how they were educated and who might be lucky enough to learn how to read. Very few people actually learned how to write, including most of the aristocracy, who used scribes to compose letters and documents for their approval.

Finally, the book will include details of "Places" that played a part in the making of Magna Carta. While Runnymede is the first that springs to mind, there are many others that must also be included. London was by far and away the largest and most important city in England, but there were new cities blossoming all over the country as trade within the country and with foreign territories expanded at a rate never before known. Merchants, tradesmen and professionals began to form a new, growing tier of society – the "middle class" – and its value to the barons is recognized in certain clauses of Magna Carta.

Yet the places highlighted in this book are not just the cathedral towns, trading ports and fortresses scattered across England. At the time of Magna Carta, there were other places – thousands of miles away and on the other side of the Atlantic – where cities that would one day revere the document had yet to be founded. In fact, some of the most important places in the Magna Carta story would not boast any settlement that could be called a city until the sixteenth century, four centuries after the English barons first put their demands to the reluctant King John.

Magna Carta was born in England, but it would come of age in the United States, where what it was originally intended to be, and to do, mattered far less than the concepts that it was taken to represent. The document was originally intended to be a peace agreement and to be used to control the excesses of the English monarch, but in the United States it was the way that the document enshrined the concepts of justice and freedom for all under the rule of law that mattered most. It is the way in which those concepts have been developed over the past 800 years that make Magna Carta of such immense significance to all of us today – even if that is a world away from what the barons intended of their historic document.

FEUDALISM

By the early thirteenth century, the population of England had grown to over 3 million, and the vast majority of people lived in the countryside. Cities were evolving at a great rate, with almost 60 new towns established in England between 1180 and 1230. King John encouraged the growth of these ports and trade centres. He founded Liverpool in 1207, inviting those who had the means to take a stake in developing this new port by leasing plots of land that had been marked out on the banks of the River Mersey. John undoubtedly saw Liverpool as an opportunity to create a new embarkation point for troops crossing to Ireland, but there were also substantial trading opportunities to exploit. Bristol had grown enormously through its trading connections with Ireland and was beginning to rival London in size.

Even London, however, more than 10 times the size of most other cities in the country, had a population of less than 80,000 – today its population is more than 100 times that size. Most people lived in a rural environment, working on the land. That's pretty much the way it would stay until the industrial age, when machines would take over much of the labour-intensive farm work, sweeping the workers off the land and into the new factories. However, as late as the beginning of the nineteenth century, only 20 per cent of Britain's entire population lived in towns.

With the nation having a mainly rural population, society was administered in a way that revolved around the land: those who worked the land and those who owned it. There was a social hierarchy enshrined in tradition and in law that ensured the poorest people would live in squalor thereby supporting the rich who lived in luxury. Known as "feudalism" in England, and across most of Europe, the system had a form that can best be described as a pyramid, with the king at the pinnacle and each tier of society stretching out beneath him. In a way, it followed the natural order of any species, with the strongest imposing his will on the less strong, and they, in turn, passing the same message down to the lower ranks.

There could be many levels to the pyramid, but to appreciate how it worked and to understand some of the terminology, we need only look at a simplified form.

When a king such as John came to power or conquered a new land, he would grant land and property to his most loyal supporters, or confirm the holdings of those in his new kingdom who were to stay in charge of lands traditionally held by their families.

In order to grant land, the king had to make his underling a "vassal" – someone who owed allegiance to the king and was in effect the "king's man". "Vassal" comes from an Old French word for "servant" and a Celtic word meaning "boy".

This occurred at a formal ritual known as a "commendation ceremony", which was broken down into two distinct parts. In the first part, the would-be vassal paid "homage" (again associated with being the king's man, *homme* being French for man) to the king, kneeling before him bareheaded in a stance that demonstrated complete submission. He then stretched out his hands, palms together, as though praying. The traditional Christian posture for prayer, kneeling with the hands pressed together, probably originates with the act of homage. Prior to this submissive pose being adopted, most people would have prayed while standing with their arms outstretched.

The vassal would then announce to everyone in attendance that he wished to become the king's man. Clasping the vassal's hands between his own, the king would declare his acceptance – this gesture was a symbol that the vassal was now part of the king's tribe and that the king's power flowed through him. The vassal promised to fight only for the king and in return he was promised the protection of the Crown.

The second part of the ceremony involved the vassal swearing "fealty" to the king (from the Latin *fidelitas*, meaning "faithfulness"). He would place one hand on a Bible, or on a holy relic, and swear before God to be loyal to the king.

A man could swear an oath of fealty to more than one person, but could only pay homage to – only promise to fight for – the king. The commendation ceremony would also involve promises from the king of land and titles, and assurances from the vassal about how many fighting men he would field in support of the king. The strength and type of military commitment would be agreed according to the extent of revenue potential from the lands granted to the vassal. As such, the ritual could be seen as a contract between the two, with guarantees made on either side that benefitted both.

A military arrangement was the most important of the vassal's guarantees to the king, but it was far from the only one. The vassal might also be required to attend the king's court, whether sitting as an advisor, providing counsel on affairs of state when the king called his noblemen together to form a parliament, or whether presiding over proceedings at his own baronial court.

The baronial court dealt with local disputes and crimes, which would be put before the vassal in order for him to pass sentence in accordance with the law. Capital punishment, or any number of gruesome penalties – including blinding and mutilation – could be inflicted on the general populace for crimes that, from our modern-day perspective, seem relatively trivial.

The feudal system cascaded down through the different strata of society. The most powerful and prominent of the king's vassals were his barons. These men held titles and lands that included several "knights' fees". These were parcels of land, usually with a substantial manor house or castle, from which a knight derived his income. As tenant-in-chief of the land awarded to him by the king, a baron could have between 12 and 20 knight's fees as part of his estates, as well as land that he held in his own right.

The knights became vassals of the barons (although a knight could be a king's vassal), and they, in turn, made vassals of the peasants who worked on their land. When paying homage, the lower ranks of vassals placed their head (instead of their hands) between their lord's hands. However, not everyone went through a commendation ceremony, and for the peasantry it was often accepted that they owed allegiance to whoever controlled the land. A peasant's lord might own everything on the land, including the peasants' livestock, their homes, the tools they used, and perhaps even the clothes that they wore.

The general principle of how feudalism worked is, therefore, quite straightforward, but it could vary in practice from one region to another and there were always a few "wild cards" that could find their way into the arrangements.

A knight's fee was calculated by his overlord to present the knight with sufficient revenue to buy arms, armour and horses, and to generally equip himself for battle. He would also be expected to maintain his own retinue of support staff and recruit men-at-arms from his estate if required. His military service would normally be for up to 40 days each year. There were, however, ways around this. A knight, or even a baron, might be permitted to pay a fee called "scutage" instead of going off to fight. The scutage money would allow his overlord to hire mercenaries should he need them.

Military service might also include "castle-guard", which involved – as the name suggests – guarding the castle of an overlord, or a royal castle, for a certain number of days each year.

The greatest of the wild cards, however, was the clergy. Church leaders, from the local priest to bishops and archbishops received money from those within their area of influence as a kind of religious tax – this was around 10 per cent of the income of everyone, from a peasant to a baron. However, clergymen could also own land in their own right, and the highest-ranking clergymen were on a par with the barony.

The clergy played an enormously important role in feudal society. They were often the only properly educated men in the area – the only ones who could read and write. In those extremely religious and extremely superstitious times, when failing to lead your life in accordance with the teachings of the Church could bring charges of heresy crashing down on your head, the clergy were to be respected and feared. While the rest of the population could trace the line of their loyalty up through their local overlord, to the baron who held his allegiance, and ultimately to the king, the clergy could look at things a little differently. They could claim that their loyalty went beyond the king to the pope, and thence to God.

It is hardly surprising, then, that a king would do his utmost to ensure that he placed men loyal to himself in positions of influence in the Church, even if that risked going against the wishes of the pope. This meant that the men in the highest religious offices were often not the most devout Christians, but the most ruthless and astute politicians who could use their status to remain close to the seat of power and to live the life of a fabulously wealthy aristocrat.

There was, of course, a separate hierarchy within the Church, where priests tended to their local congregations but were subordinate to bishops, then archbishops and ultimately (here on Earth, at least), the pope. The clergy collected their own taxes, known as "tithes", from the local populace, a tithe representing one tenth of a man's income, but land and property were also donated or bequeathed to the Church, as well as being awarded by the king to his favourites.

To appreciate the extent of the feudal system in England, we need only look at how the Normans imposed themselves on society after invading in 1066 and defeating the Anglo-Saxon King Harold. At the time of the invasion, it is estimated that there were around 4,500 Anglo-Saxon aristocrats who owned most of the land and property in the country. By 1086, when the Domesday Book was compiled, the pyramid of power descended from the king to 180 barons, who held land directly from the king and were known as "tenants-in-chief". Below the barons were around 1,400 lesser tenants, minor nobles, knights or other titled aristocrats, holding land from the barons. Below them were sub-tenants, who held land under lease – land that they may have owned previously – that covered 6,000 or so small estates.

As far as King John was concerned, the entire chain of ownership existed to channel wealth upwards to him, to be used as he pleased – and what gratified him most was planning to recover the vast estates that had been taken from him on the other side of the English Channel.

ELEANOR OF AQUITAINE

Although she died 11 years before Magna Carta came into being, Eleanor of Aquitaine is one of the most important characters in its story. Through marriage, motherhood and her own time spent administering the throne of England, Eleanor was integral to the development of the circumstances leading to the conference at Runnymede. Beautiful, elegant, highly intelligent, ambitious and ruthless, Eleanor was matriarch of a family that was responsible for much of the political unrest throughout Europe – turmoil that brought her son, King John, to the negotiating table in 1215.

It is easy to assume that, in a medieval world dominated by men, women had no control over their own destiny. To suit the political or financial ambitions of her father, a young girl could be promised in marriage practically from birth, although the Church had decreed that the minimum age at which a girl could actually be married was 12. Young ladies of noble birth generally received very little formal education but were, instead, trained to run a household, deal with servants and the practical business of ensuring that there was a fire in the hearth and food on the table, just as their husbands expected. Women were also expected to produce children, preferably boys who would grow up to inherit their father's wealth.

It is not entirely accurate, however, to say no women had control over their lives. The daughters of rich and powerful men could inherit land or property and some women, through circumstance or through strength of character, were able to acquire great wealth and power in their own right. Eleanor of Aquitaine was one such woman – an extraordinary character who placed her own family, her children and her ancestral lands above the wishes of her husbands, even though both of those were powerful kings.

Born in 1122, in the Duchy of Aquitaine, Eleanor was brought up on spellbinding tales of her family's adventures, especially those of her grandfather, William IX of Aquitaine. William, a big man with a fiery temper, was a warrior and a renowned poet who loved to scandalize his audiences. He was never one to let tradition, custom or even the law stand in his way. He divorced his first wife, Ermengarde, and married again, his second wife, Philippa, giving him seven children before he fell in love with Dangereuse de l'Isle Bouchard, wife of the Viscount of Châtellerault.

Dangereuse, it seems, had not earned her risky name lightly and was so called because of her beguiling, seductive manner. She appears to have been a willing participant when William decided to kidnap her while visiting the viscount. He spirited Dangereuse off to his palace in Poitiers and installed her in the tower which was the living quarters of his immediate family. This kind of abduction wasn't unheard of among the nobility in medieval Europe – however, that didn't mean that William's wife was best pleased when she returned from a visit to her family in Toulouse to find another woman in her home. Eventually, she left William; later, she was instrumental in getting the pope to excommunicate both William and Dangereuse from the Church.

William, however, was a very rich and powerful man and eventually persuaded the pope to allow him back into the Church. Aenor, Dangereuse's daughter from her previous marriage ultimately married William's son, also called William, and it was from this union that Eleanor of Aquitaine came into the world.

Such a colourful and turbulent family history might suggest that Eleanor lived in a world of chaos and debauchery, but she was, in fact, brought up in the sedate splendour of the mighty

Palace of Poitiers. Since Poitiers was a hugely influential centre for culture and the arts, young Eleanor would have been entertained by the finest musicians, poets, actors, acrobats and puppeteers in Europe. As part of her education as a lady, Eleanor was taught needlework, spinning and weaving but, unlike many girls of her social standing, her education also stretched into the academic realm. William made sure that his daughter was taught arithmetic, astronomy and history, as well as how to read Latin and her local Poitevin – although she probably never learned to write.

The palace would have been a busy place with a huge variety of people coming and going. Eleanor learned how to deal with the army of servants and staff required to keep a large house functioning smoothly, most probably being taught alongside other girls from lesser aristocratic families who had been sent to Poitiers to learn such accomplishments. Taught how to play the harp and to dance, Eleanor also mastered the skills of riding, hawking and hunting. She even learnt how to play chess, a game that had been known in Europe for a century or so but had been growing in popularity since the pieces started to be represented as kings, queens and men-at-arms. Unusually for a girl, from a relatively young age Eleanor was also introduced to the grown-up world of power politics.

As the administrative centre for a duchy that covered half of what is now France, the palace would have received many visitors from far and wide, some bearing tales of treachery or villainy which the duke was expected to act upon. Eleanor's father, like his father before him, journeyed the length and breadth of his territory at least once a year with a travelling court, establishing himself in the castles of his noblemen to collect rents and taxes, settle disputes and administer justice. When she was only seven, Eleanor witnessed a legal document in Montierneuf Abbey, making her mark on the parchment alongside her name and taking her first step into the world of politics.

Eleanor was, therefore, very much aware of life outside the palace, absorbing ever more knowledge about the ways of the world as she learned how her father put down rebellions and repelled invaders. Alongside the performing arts she also learned something of the art of war.

In 1130, Eleanor's mother, Aenor, and her younger brother, William, both fell ill and died. Her mother was only 27 years old and her brother just 4. As Eleanor had only one other sibling, her younger sister, Petronilla, she was now heir to the Duchy of Aquitaine. Eleanor's father was encouraged to take another wife in order to produce a male heir, and even went as far as arranging to marry Emma, Countess of Limoges. However, William's enemies, unwilling to allow him to extend his power, kidnapped Emma and married her off to the Count of Angoulême.

William's quarrels were not just with his noblemen, but also with the Church. He backed the wrong pope, supporting Antipope Anacletus II instead of the ultimate pope, Innocent II, and banishing Innocent II's supporters from Aquitaine. William was excommunicated for his trouble but, like his father, was eventually reconciled with the Church. In 1137, he undertook a pilgrimage to Santiago de Compostela, in Spain. Eleanor and Petronilla accompanied him as far as Bordeaux, where William left them in the care of the archbishop, who was a loyal friend.

William fell ill on his journey to Spain and, realizing that he was dying, made a will naming Eleanor as his heir. He named King Louis VI of France as her protector, entrusting him to administer the Duchy of Aquitaine until the 15-year-old Eleanor was old enough to take charge. When King Louis received this news, he was also gravely ill, but swiftly arranged for Eleanor to marry his own son – also called Louis

– hoping that this would bring the duchy under royal control once and for all.

Eleanor was married to the 16-year-old Louis in Bordeaux in July 1137. Things did not, however, go entirely as King Louis might have liked. As part of the marriage agreement, Eleanor's lands were to remain separate from those of the French Crown until such time as Eleanor had a son, who would ultimately become both Duke of Aquitaine and King of France. Eleanor was defending her family's ancestral lands.

A few weeks after the wedding, King Louis died and his son became King Louis VII and Eleanor, Queen of France. The couple travelled to Paris where they began to make improvements to many of the city's buildings, especially the grim Cité Palace that was to be Eleanor's new home. The new queen also brought her entertainers and artists to brighten up staid Parisian society, leading to accusations that she was leading an outrageously extravagant, self-indulgent and probably adulterous lifestyle. This was the sort of gossip that the king's political enemies could easily use against him.

When Petronilla began an affair with a far older, married man, Eleanor persuaded the king to help have the man's marriage annulled. This caused a huge uproar and led to armed conflict between forces loyal to the king and the relatives of the abandoned wife. Louis personally led an assault on the town of Vitry, which resulted in a church being burned to the ground and the deaths of 1,000 people sheltering inside. Eleanor was clearly able to influence King Louis, and those who would rather that power rested in their hands did their best to drive the royal couple apart.

Despite an increasingly turbulent relationship, Eleanor and Louis had a daughter, Marie, in 1145. In 1147, anxious to make amends for the burning of the church, Louis agreed to embark on a crusade to Jerusalem, where the Holy City was under threat from Turkish Muslim forces. Eleanor decided that she, too, would join the crusade, not least because her uncle, Raymond of Poitiers, prince of the crusader kingdom of Antioch, had pleaded for military aid to protect him from the Turks. She recruited an army from Aquitaine and travelled with the crusader force, along with a huge retinue of servants and ladies-in-waiting. Eleanor would be gone for two-and-a-half years, leaving Marie behind in France.

The crusade – which involved, amongst others, around 15,000 French and 20,000 German troops – was a military disaster and contributed to the Christians eventually losing control of Jerusalem. Eleanor and Louis argued over how their forces should be deployed, falling out to such an extent that she demanded that their marriage be annulled. They visited the pope on their way home to Paris and he persuaded them to persevere with their marriage. In 1150, Eleanor gave birth to another daughter, Alix, yet all was not well in this marriage. Louis wanted a son, and Eleanor had grown weary of her husband, whom she saw as weak and now overly devout. In 1152, they finally divorced.

Eleanor's daughters, who were, after all, royal princesses, stayed with their father in Paris while Eleanor returned to Aquitaine. Within weeks she married Henry, Duke of Normandy and Count of Anjou. A swift marriage to Henry, who was 11 years younger and a distant cousin, was a wise move. There had been two attempts to kidnap Eleanor as she returned to Aquitaine, one masterminded by Henry's younger brother, Geoffrey. The kidnappers' intent was to marry her, whether she wanted it or not, and seize control of Aquitaine. Eleanor, however, had met Henry when he came to Paris to pledge allegiance to her former husband. She admired him: he was a bold, strong young man – just the person to rule Aquitaine by her side. Together, in fact, Henry and Eleanor owned land that stretched half the length of the English Channel and all the way down the Atlantic coast to the border with Spain, and inland most of the way to the Mediterranean. Eleanor was now the most powerful woman in Europe but Henry had further ambitions.

Henry harboured a claim to the throne of England. Encouraged by Eleanor, he led a force across the Channel in 1153, revisiting the dispute with King Stephen over his right to the throne – an argument that had been raging ever since the death of Henry's grandfather, King Henry I, in 1135. Henry's mother, Matilda, had tried to press her claim to the English throne and had seized control of the south west of the country, but the war had ultimately ground to a stalemate. Henry and Stephen came to an agreement towards the end of 1153 – when Stephen died, he would name Henry as his heir rather than any of his own sons. This happened sooner than anyone expected when Stephen became terminally ill in 1154. Henry became king and Eleanor, the former Queen of France, was now Queen of England.

Henry and Eleanor were crowned in Westminster Abbey, London, Eleanor heavily pregnant with their second son, Henry. Their first son, William, had been born the previous year. Altogether, Eleanor had 10 children. There were two daughters, Marie (1145–98) and Alix (1150–97) by Louis VII; and five sons and three daughters by Henry II: William (1153–56), Henry (1155–83), Matilda (1156–89), Richard (1157–99), Geoffrey (1158–86), Eleanor (1161–1214), Joanna (1165–99) and John (1166–1216). All of the children, except Eleanor and John, died before their mother.

Three of Eleanor's sons became kings, two of her daughters became queens and the family's descendants populated the ruling classes across Europe. Eleanor herself ruled the kingdom when Henry was absent dealing with problems on the other side of the Channel. She convened courts throughout England, settling disputes and issuing charters on behalf of her husband. Nevertheless, Eleanor's family life was far from harmonious.

By the time her youngest son, John, was two years old, Eleanor and her husband had separated. Eleanor returned to Aquitaine to rule over the duchy, while Henry concentrated on maintaining his English throne and conducting violent disputes with rebellious vassals, as well as longstanding territorial disputes with the French King Louis VII.

Although he granted his sons titles and honours, King Henry retained a firm grip on the reins of power. To try to keep his growing sons on side, in 1173, Henry crowned his eldest surviving son, also called Henry, joint King of England. This remains the only time that England had two official kings. To avoid confusion with his father, the newly crowned 18-year-old was known as "Henry The Young King".

Despite this, Eleanor was convinced that her husband was intent on denying her sons their birthright, and she supported her boys in various rebellions against their father. Showing how dysfunctional the family had become, at any one time, Henry would side with one son against another in order to put down these uprisings. Some of this family discord may have originated in Eleanor's fear that Henry's illegitmate sons might one day challenge her sons' rightful inheritance.

In 1174, Eleanor and her sons were defeated, following an abortive attempt to overthrow Henry, backed by Louis VII, her former husband. Henry forgave his sons, but placed Eleanor under house arrest at Old Sarum Castle in Salisbury, where she remained for the next 15 years. When Henry The Young King pleaded for her release, as he lay dying of dysentery in Limousin during his campaign against his father, Henry and his brother, Richard, in 1183, the former refused.

Eleanor was permitted to leave her prison from time to time, however. Henry even took her to Normandy, in 1185, to instruct Richard, Eleanor's favourite son, to agree to Henry's terms for settling their dispute, after he had sided with Louis VII in a war against his father. The squabbles over who would succeed Henry raged on until he died in 1189. Geoffrey had died three years previously, trampled by horses at a tournament in Paris, leaving the way clear for Richard to take the English throne.

In fact, Eleanor played a greater role in ruling England than her son. Richard had no wife and his mother ruled as Queen Regent for two months while he was invested as Duke of Normandy before being crowned in Westminster Abbey on 3 September 1189. Eleanor continued to be heavily involved as Richard then spent much of his time preparing for the Third Crusade. He departed in the summer of 1190, and just as she had done when ruling alongside Henry, Eleanor took care of Richard's affairs while he was gone.

Taking care of business included preventing her youngest son, John, from seizing the throne, supported as he was by Philip II, son of Eleanor's first husband and King of France since Louis's death, in 1180. It also included finding Richard a wife, and Eleanor chose a Spanish aristocrat, Berengaria of Navarre. This was an ideal political match since Berengaria's territory would secure the southern border of Aquitaine. The arrangement completely ignored the fact that Richard was already promised to Alys, sister of Philip II.

At the age of 69, Eleanor made the journey south across Europe, through the Pyrenees, to collect Berengaria and escort her to Richard, who was then in Sicily. It was a huge distance to travel and demonstrates Eleanor's enduring energy, but it was far from being the final long journey that Eleanor would undertake. When Richard, on his way home from the crusade in 1193, was captured by Henry VI, the German king and Holy Roman Emperor, Eleanor raised the required ransom and took it to Germany.

Eleanor returned to Aquitaine and, having persuaded her two surviving sons to settle their differences, retired to Fontevrault Abbey in the Loire Valley. In 1199, news came that

Richard had been wounded during a siege in the Limousin. Eleanor rushed to be by the side of her son as he died.

Richard had named John as heir to his throne and titles. Eleanor toured Aquitaine to ensure support for John, travelling once again to Spain in 1200 to bring back her 12-year-old granddaughter, Blanche, as a bride for John. Exhausted, Eleanor made it only as far as Fontevrault, before entrusting final delivery of Blanche to the Archbishop of Bordeaux.

Two years later, war broke out once again between John and Philip II. Eleanor's 15-year-old grandson (the son of Geoffrey) was backed by Philip, who wanted to wrest land and the English throne from John. Eleanor declared her support for John and headed for Poitiers to prevent Arthur seizing the capital of Aquitaine. Arthur's forces trapped and besieged his grandmother at the castle of Mirabeau. Eleanor held out until John's forces fought their way south, capturing Arthur and lifting the siege.

Now frail and unwell, Eleanor returned to the abbey at Fontevrault, where she remained until her death in 1204 at the age of 82.

 # THE ARTICLES OF THE BARONS

There was no Magna Carta at Runnymede – that document would be drawn up later. The document to which King John attached his Great Seal at Runnymede was the barons' list of demands, known as The Articles of the Barons.

Contrary to popular opinion and to the scenes that have been portrayed in countless paintings and illustrations over the centuries – where a morose John, looking cowed and threatened, sits, quill in hand, appending his name to Magna

Carta – the king did not actually sign documents. In fact, the king probably couldn't write. A document became official when the king attached his seal, stamping an embossment into a mixture of hot wax and resin which adhered to a tape threaded through a slit in the document.

The Articles of the Barons (currently held in the British Library, London) was originally headed "These are the clauses that the barons seek and the lord concedes" and was divided into two sections. The first was an orderly list of 48 paragraphs outlining the demands of the barons. These demands, after many days of negotiation, changes, qualifications and additions, were to become Magna Carta, although at that time known either as the Charter of Liberties or the Charter of Runnymede. The name "Magna Carta" was adopted when the charter was reissued by John's son, Henry III, in 1217.

Versions of all of the demands appear as clauses in Magna Carta, although there is no direct equivalent of the barons' Paragraph 13. This demand refers to court hearings that are essentially covered in expanded detail in Clause 18.

The list of demands ends with a call for the rights issued by the king under the charter to be granted to all of England's landowners. This became Clause 60 of Magna Carta.

The second section of the document deals with the way the rights granted will be guaranteed, mentions the committee of 25 barons and confirms that the king will not renege on the agreement, issues that were dealt with in the latter clauses of Magna Carta.

There are six clauses of Magna Carta that have no direct equivalent in The Articles of the Barons – Clauses 1, 14, 19, 21, 24 and 57.

- **Clause 1** deals with the freedom of the Church and its right to elect its own officials, something that had apparently been agreed before the conference at Runnymede.

- **Clause 14** is concerned with the way that a parliament would be convened to discuss and to agree the levying of taxes.
- **Clause 19** requires that men of sufficient rank and responsibility should make themselves available for court duties to deal with legal disputes or criminal issues thus ensuring that justice was done and the law properly administered in a timely manner.
- **Clause 21** ensures that the nobility can only be tried and punished by those of equal rank.
- **Clause 24** makes it clear that local court officials can not sit in judgement on matters that are beyond their responsibility.
- **Clause 57** promises the return of any land and property that the Plantagenet kings appropriated from the Welsh.

The Articles of the Barons was kept secure by Stephen Langton, the Archbishop of Canterbury, who had helped the barons to compose their list of demands. He stored it in the archives at Lambeth Palace, London. The palace was looted in the middle of the seventeenth century but remarkably the document survived intact and in legible condition until it was acquired by the British Library.

 # HENRY II, KING OF ENGLAND

The titles accorded to Henry II reflect the prestige, power and wealth that came with the vast tracts of land that he held not only in England, Wales and Ireland, but also in over half of what is now France. He was Count of Anjou, Count of Maine, Duke of Normandy, Duke of Aquitaine, Count of Nantes... and the list goes on. He became King of England in 1154, having mounted a military campaign against King Stephen in pursuit of his claim to the Crown as grandson of Henry I. Shortly before his death, Stephen finally named Henry as his heir.

Henry is known as the first of the Angevin Kings, the name coming from his title as Count of Anjou (a province now in France, centred around the town of Angers). The other two Angevin Kings were his sons, Richard and John, also known by Henry's family name of "Plantagenet". Henry realized that he could not hold his vast empire together by force of will or sheer brute force – although that was a final option to which he defaulted regularly. He was keen to devolve some of the responsibilities of administration, especially when it came to maintaining law and order.

In England, Henry introduced wide-ranging innovations in the way that court cases were heard, sending Royal Justices to all of the counties of England to hear both civil and criminal cases in order that justice could be administered more swiftly in local courts. He also came down hard on crime, confiscating the belongings of thieves and other criminals, and introduced trial by jury – although trial by combat (where two parties could fight it out or nominate champions to fight on their behalf), and trial by ordeal (if you survived the torture you were innocent, or perhaps guilty depending on how the ordeal was being judged) remained in use.

Henry made determined efforts to introduce such civilizing reforms not only in England, but also in his territories on the other side of the Channel. In fact, many of the innovations introduced in England had first been seen in Normandy. While all of this sounds as if Henry had ambitions to rule as a philanthropic monarch bent on reforming government and achieving peace and prosperity throughout his realm, it should be noted that he would not have been able to make these changes without being ruthlessly ambitious.

Henry was swift to clamp down militarily on any signs of rebellion anywhere in his kingdom, from the territories in the very southwest of France to the border with Scotland in the far north.

He spent most of his reign extending his holdings in France, often at the expense of his long-time rival, the French King Philip II – whose wife, Eleanor of Aquitaine, Henry had married with almost indecent haste just eight weeks after Philip had their marriage annulled. Marrying Eleanor, of course, brought the vast territories of Aquitaine under Henry's control, which certainly vexed Philip.

Henry had eight children with Eleanor, five of them sons. His first son, William, died as an infant, but the others all became something of a problem for him, sometimes individually, and sometimes in collaboration with one another. His sons' grievances revolved around the land and titles they would ultimately inherit. It was clear that Henry's oldest son, also called Henry, would succeed him as King of England – or was it? Henry had an illegitimate son, Geoffrey, who had been born a year before William. While he did not have a clear right to the throne, he might try to snatch at least part of the legitimate boys' inheritance, as might another illegitimate son, also, rather confusingly, named William.

To try to keep his sons happy, Henry bestowed titles upon them. In 1170, he made his oldest son, 15-year-old Henry, "joint king". He gave "Henry the Young King" no power and eventually he rebelled. He died of dysentery in France in 1183, while leading a mercenary army against his father and his younger brother and Henry's favourite son, Richard.

Tall, good-looking, athletic and a natural warrior, Richard was encouraged by his mother to take up arms against his father. His brother Geoffrey – and occasionally his youngest brother, John – joined him. Richard eventually made peace with his father, but only after Henry had raised an army of thousands of mercenaries to subdue the forces ranged against him.

Geoffrey had participated in the revolt against his father and, like his older brother, he was granted lands and property once he agreed to behave. Unfortunately, he died at a tournament in Paris in 1186.

That left John, the youngest son, who stood to inherit least and was consequently nicknamed "Lackland" by his father. In fact, John would take – and lose – everything.

 # RUNNYMEDE

Today, Runnymede is an open stretch of grassy meadow running alongside the River Thames, from the M25 motorway northwest towards Old Windsor. With pleasure cruisers making their way sedately up and down the river, it is a peaceful spot and popular for family picnics – if you discount the noise from the passenger jets flying in and out of London's Heathrow Airport.

There are a number of memorials at Runnymede. High on Cooper's Hill, shielded from the vale by a small woodland, is the Commonwealth Air Forces Memorial, commemorating the men and women of the Allied air forces who died during the Second World War and recording the names of more than 20,000 airmen who have no known graves.

Further west and lower down the slope is the official British memorial to US President John F. Kennedy, a 7-ton block of Portland stone inscribed with a quote from the president's inaugural address:

"Let every nation know, whether it wishes us well or ill, that we shall pay any price, bear any burden, meet any hardship, support any friend or oppose any foe, in order to assure the survival and success of liberty."

The acre of ground in which the memorial sits was gifted by the British people to the people of the United States and the memorial was dedicated in May 1965 at a ceremony attended by Queen Elizabeth II and Jacqueline Kennedy, held before a formal reception at Windsor Castle.

Between those two memorials sits another, also with an American connection. In 1957, the lawyers of the American Bar Association commissioned a neoclassical monument to commemorate a landmark in history that happened before the United States even existed. Beneath a small, flat-domed pavilion set in lawns shaded by trees, sits a pillar of stone that bears the legend: "To commemorate Magna Carta, symbol of Freedom Under Law."

This elegant area of landscaping looks out over the spot where, 800 years ago, King John met with the rebel barons to negotiate the terms on which Magna Carta is based. Why here? There is a clue in the name, if you look back far enough. The name "Runnymede" is derived from Anglo-Saxon words "runieg", which means regular meeting, and "mede" meaning meadow. Runnymede was, therefore, an important site for meetings long before King John and the barons chose it for their rendezvous.

There are, of course, many other places that could have been used for this significant occasion. The king had met previously with the barons at the Temple Church in London, for example, but, with both sides on a war footing, this was a "safe" place to meet.

The barons' forces were camped at Staines, and beyond Staines they held London. They were heavily armed and prepared to go into battle. The king's men were gathered around Windsor Castle, a near-impregnable fortress close enough for the king to flee to should the need arise, but also a formidable base from which to launch an attack. Yet meeting at Runnymede meant that a pitched battle was out of the question.

The meadow at that time was not a place that could easily be accessed by a formation of horsemen, or even formations of foot soldiers. Sandwiched between a ridge and the river, there was no room for manoeuvre on the way in. The flat area of the meadow itself might seem like the perfect battlefield, but the ground is very wet and the knights' heavy horses would have sunk in, slithered around and, if they could make any progress at all, would have turned the place into a quagmire in no time. For all of these reasons, Runnymede had become a meeting place long before Magna Carta.

Today, in a place so revered by the people of the United States, we have an American woman to thank for it being open for everyone to enjoy. Cara Leland Rogers Broughton, Lady Fairhaven –the wife of English civil engineer Urban Broughton – gifted the area to the National Trust in 1929.

 # KING JOHN

John could never have expected to become king. He was the youngest son and youngest child of Henry and Eleanor of Aquitaine and must have felt more like an orphan than an English prince when he was growing up at Fontevrault Abbey. His parents were living separate lives – his mother was raising support from among her noblemen in Anjou and scheming against her husband and his father was crushing all opposition. Neither paid much attention to the youngest of their brood.

This wasn't too out of the ordinary for a dynastic family, and children were often raised by a series of nurses, teachers and guardians. When he was old enough, John spent some time at the court of his eldest brother, Henry the Young King, learning about chivalry and the military arts. However, unlike his older brother, Richard, John wasn't really cut out to be a great warrior.

As a grown man, Richard is thought to have been about 6 feet 3 inches tall (1.9 metres) and John, at 5 feet 5 inches (1.68 metres), would barely have come up to his shoulder. Richard was handsome, with strong limbs and red-gold hair, while John was shifty-looking, with much darker red hair – although he was still said to have a strong, stocky build. In that respect, John was like his father, Henry II, who was also broad and powerful.

In fact, Henry II's sons came in all shapes and sizes. Like Richard, Henry the Young King was tall, strong and a tournament hero, while Henry's third son, Geoffrey, was similar in stature to himself. One of Henry's illegitimate sons, William, Earl of Salisbury, was even bigger than Richard.

Whether John envied his taller brothers their athleticism or not, it can be fairly certain that he did covet their lands and titles. Henry the Young King was crowned joint King of England alongside his father when he was just 15, although he was given very little power and would later rebel against his father in an attempt to establish himself in at least some of the territories of which he was nominal overlord. He was to die campaigning against Henry in 1183.

That of course, made Richard the heir to the throne. Richard and John's other elder brother, Geoffrey, had been part of a rebellion against their father in 1173, rallying support from disaffected barons in England, malcontent vassals in Aquitaine, the French King Louis VII and the King of Scotland, William the Lion. Their father put down the revolt and during the conflict, John – then just seven years old – was with his father. Henry began to look upon John as a favourite son.

Previously, Henry had nicknamed his youngest son "Lackland" because his other sons had all, ostensibly, been given lands and titles. However, John now began to come into his own. Henry seized estates in Cornwall to give to John and arranged for him to marry Isabella of Gloucester, which would bring John even more land. In 1177, Henry made John, then just 11 years old, Lord of Ireland. When Henry the Young King died in 1183, Henry made John Duke of Aquitaine, a title that was intended to go to Richard. This sparked another war between Richard and Henry, with Geoffrey and John this time on their father's side.

By 1185, with the war over, John was sent on his first trip to Ireland in order to try to play the diplomat with the Irish nobles, who were severely perturbed at having been subdued by an Anglo-Norman invasion. The situation was tense, and John did nothing to help matters by laughing at the Irish lords, whose beards and long hair seemed unfashionable compared to the noblemen at his father's court in England (who had adopted shorter haircuts and a clean-shaven appearance). It was a brash, insensitive and insulting thing to do, but such behaviour was to become habitual for John.

John could often be charming, witty and generous and he was an attentive host. (At times, perhaps, a little too attentive – when he became king he had a reputation for seducing, or attempting to seduce, his noblemen's wives.) However, he was also reported to have an explosive and vicious temper, doubtless fuelled by his fondness for wine, which could leave him snarling in fits of rage. Given that he also had a reputation for sadistic cruelty, no one was really safe when King John blew his top.

Yet was the rage and cruelty so unusual? His older brother, the noble Richard the Lionheart, has gone down in history – or at least in folklore – as a chivalrous hero, yet the punishment he had written into his forest laws for poaching the king's deer was for the poacher to be blinded and castrated. These were cruel and barbarous times when the law deemed it a fitting punishment for a man to be tied to a stake in front of a bonfire, slit open and disembowelled, his intestines thrown onto the bonfire, while the victim was still alive to see it happening. He might then have all of his limbs hacked off as his body was "quartered". If you can think of a horrific way to torture someone to death, you can be pretty sure that someone in the Middle Ages had already thought of it and tried it out.

Neither was it uncommon for someone in John's position to exhibit bouts of temper. Noblemen were used to getting their own way. Kings simply expected it. Again, John's older brother, Richard, can be taken as an example. When Saladin failed to meet his demands, after Richard had captured the city of Acre in the Holy Land in 1191, Richard was furious and ordered the execution of almost 3,000 Muslim prisoners on a hill not far from the city, in full view of Saladin's army. Repeated attempts to charge the hill and save the prisoners were beaten back while the massacre continued.

John may not have been much like Richard in a physical sense, but there was certainly a nasty temper and a cruel streak that ran in their blood.

When Geoffrey died at a tournament in France in 1186, there was another reshuffling of titles and Richard, preparing to go off on a crusade, began to worry that, should anything happen to his father, John might be named as his successor instead of him. This anxiety became the source of another war between father and son, with Henry's old enemy Louis VII of France supporting Richard. By 1189, the family was at peace again, with Richard confirmed as Henry's heir. Henry died in that year, and Richard became king and immediately started raising funds for his crusade, leaving in the summer of 1190.

While he was away and his mother, Eleanor, was busy on the other side of the channel holding the Angevin Empire together, Richard's chancellor, William Longchamp, Bishop of Ely ran the country, along with Bishop Hugh de Puiset and William de Mandeville.

When Mandeville died, Longchamp began to abuse his position, refusing to work with Puiset and assuming dangerous levels of power. All of this caused unrest among the barons and the clergy. John, who had agreed with Richard that he would stay out of England until Richard's return, now took the opportunity to re-enter the country in order to restrain Longchamp. The situation soon deteriorated into armed conflict but ended with John being welcomed into London as a hero in 1191. The London lords and merchants were a powerful political force, having been granted various rights and freedoms, yet Longchamp upset them by refusing to talk to them in English and spoke only French or Latin. Had London's leaders ever had the opportunity to talk with King Richard, they would quickly have realized that the King couldn't speak English at all.

John was clever enough to appreciate the power that the wealth of London generated and, in 1215, he would reaffirm all of the rights that London held as its own in a special charter and guarantee them in Magna Carta. London (see Clauses 12 and 13) is the only city to merit a specific reference.

With John demanding to be recognized as Richard's eventual successor and attempting to come to an arrangement with King Philip II of France over lands on the other side of the Channel, mistrust among Richard's supporters grew until fighting inevitably broke out. The conflict intensified when it was heard that Richard was on his way back to England and John finally called for a truce. When Richard arrived, John's forces surrendered and he fled to Normandy.

The brothers were eventually reconciled and John led

several campaigns in France to regain castles and territories lost to Philip II while Richard had been away on crusade. Richard named John as his successor (previously he had said it should be his nephew, Arthur of Brittany), and John finally became king when Richard was killed suppressing a revolt in Limousin in France.

Although John was crowned in Westminster Abbey and inherited all of his brother's lands and titles, his 15-year-old nephew, Arthur of Brittany, disputed his claim to the throne. He launched attacks on the Angevin Empire in France, with the support of King Philip II and backed by nobles from throughout John's territories. John went from his coronation straight to war in France, where the conflict raged until May 1200, when John agreed terms with Philip. The French king agreed to recognize John as the rightful heir to all of Richard's territories in France, while John agreed that Philip was the rightful overlord of all of those lands. Thus, the King of England became a vassal of the King of France, at least as far as his continental possessions were concerned.

The peace lasted until John decided to marry Isabella of Angoulême, abandoning his erstwhile wife, Isabella of Gloucester, and having that marriage annulled on the grounds of consanguinity (that they were too closely related). The territory that this new marriage brought to John helped to secure the eastern area of his Angevin lands, but it left many people more than a little upset, not least Hugh IX de Lusignan, to whom Isabella had been engaged. The situation between the two disintegrated into armed conflict and Philip II, as John's feudal overlord, summoned him to court in Paris in 1201. John refused to go and Philip promptly assigned all of John's feudal territories to Arthur of Brittany. There followed another continental war that raged until 1204 and further blackened John's reputation in France when he captured Arthur and his commanders at the battle of

Mirebeau. Arthur was never seen again and stories circulated that, having held him prisoner, John murdered Arthur one night in a drunken rage.

John lost many local allies through his attitude not only towards prisoners but also towards those who were fighting on his behalf. Clearly the lack of diplomacy that he had displayed in Ireland was still lacking almost 20 years later. Under pressure from Philip, John retreated to England. He lost all of the lands that his family had held on the Continent bar the Duchy of Aquitaine and would spend the rest of his life trying to win them back.

It was John's obsession with raising money to fight Philip and reclaim Normandy and his French territories that led him into such conflict at home in England. While he did attend to the running of the country and proved to be a capable administrator, he was equally capable of abusing his power in order to squeeze as much money out of his subjects as he possibly could. It took him almost 10 years to put himself in a position from which he could launch another campaign in France, but the attempt ended in defeat at the battle of Bouvines and John returned to a frosty reception in England in October 1214.

Growing unrest among the barons created by John's crippling taxes, his dispute with the pope which had caused huge distress among the population on the barons' estates, and the way in which John had installed cronies in key political and administrative positions – as well as in the Church – finally led to the barons taking military action against their king.

The rebel forces met at Northampton in May, renounced their feudal oaths to John and marched on London, which they took without a struggle. At the beginning of June, a peace conference was convened at Runnymede and the barons presented their terms during a series of meetings, culminating in the historic agreement on 15 June 1215 that came to be known as Magna Carta.

Neither side kept to the agreement. As soon as the rebels had surrendered London, John appealed to the pope to quash Magna Carta and the war raged once more, with the barons inviting Prince Louis of France to lend his support. While the war ebbed and flowed over the following year – with many of the rebel barons ultimately deciding that Louis was not the man to be their king and deserting to the royalist cause – by October 1216, John had still not managed to retake control of his kingdom. Around this time, he contracted dysentery and grew steadily weaker, dying in Newark Castle on the night of 18 October.

With John gone, more of the rebels switched sides, supporting William the Marshal as regent to John's son, the nine-year-old Henry III. One of William's first acts as regent was to reissue Magna Carta, spelling the end for Louis and his remaining supporters – although the war would continue until a peace treaty was finally signed on 12 September 1217.

 POPE INNOCENT III

Although some of Pope Innocent III's most powerful English clergy certainly played a part in bringing about Magna Carta, the pope's contribution to this historic document was to declare it invalid. When King John appealed to the pope to quash the charter, claiming that he had been forced to agree to the terms under duress, Pope Innocent III sent a letter in August 1215 condemning the charter as "shameful and demeaning" while at the same time being "unlawful and unjust." Innocent pronounced Magna Carta "void of all validity for ever", supporting King John but also giving both sides all the justification they needed to plunge England into civil war.

The man who became pope was born Lotario dei Conti di Segni around 1160 in Gavignano, close to Rome, into a wealthy and powerful Italian family. His father was Count Trasimund of Segni, a member of the house of Conti, which produced several popes. It was Lotario's uncle, Pope Clement III, who persuaded King John's father, Henry II, to support the Third Crusade – the crusade on which John's older brother, King Richard I (Richard the Lionheart), embarked following their father's death.

Educated initially in Rome, Lotario also studied in Paris before returning to Rome in the early 1180s to serve in a variety of roles under several popes, including his uncle. He became an expert in canon law and would later use this to his advantage in consolidating the power of the Catholic Church throughout Europe.

Lotario was elected pope in 1198 after Pope Celestine III died at the grand old age of 92. As Pope Innocent III, Lotario imposed his office on heads of state all over Europe, reminding them that they ruled by the grace of God, that grace being bestowed on them via the Church. In his war on heresy, he called for a crusade against the Cathars, a Christian religious sect in southwest France that had rejected the teachings of the Catholic Church. Pope Innocent III offered control of all of the lands owned by the Cathars to whoever was willing to take up arms against them. The campaign was led by Simon de Montfort and resulted in the slaughter of 20,000 people.

To impose his authority over kings, princes, noblemen and the aristocracy of Europe, Pope Innocent III would excommunicate individuals and impose interdicts that denied certain families, groups or even a whole country, access to the Church. Such an interdict was imposed on King John and the whole of England in 1208, when he refused to accept the

Pope's man, Stephen Langton, as Archbishop of Canterbury. This meant that Catholic clergy could not officiate at any religious ceremonies, thus obstructing mass and marriage rites, although the dying were still permitted to receive the last rites. While this was a major worry for some of the population, others took it less seriously. King John even managed to turn a profit during the six years of the Papal Interdict, confiscating revenues from church estates, before he finally made peace with Rome.

Pope Innocent also called for a Fourth Crusade to recapture Jerusalem from Muslim forces and imposed a "crusade tax" on all of his clergy, who had to pay one-fortieth of their annual income to raise the money needed to finance the expedition. Innocent even harboured notions of leading the crusade himself, but it is just as well that did not happen, as the whole venture went disastrously wrong, resulting in the sack of Constantinople. Only a fraction of Innocent's crusaders ever actually made it to the Holy Land and Jerusalem remained in Muslim hands.

In his favour, Innocent did preside over the Fourth Council of the Lateran in 1215, which banned the clergy from participating in any trial by ordeal. In such a trial, an accused person might be subjected to, for example, drowning to determine if he or she was innocent or guilty. If the accused survived, it was seen as a judgement from God who had intervened to save an innocent life – although sometimes the life-or-death scenario could be interpreted differently and survival could be taken as a sign that the accused was using magic or was otherwise in league with the devil. That, of course, resulted in death, anyway. The ban helped to make trial by ordeal a less frequent occurrence, but was not a realistic representation of a more merciful church, as witnessed by the horrific methods used by the Inquisition in rooting out heretics.

The Fourth Council also approved the Fifth Crusade, setting a date for its commencement in 1217. However, Innocent would not see another crusade take place. He died in Perugia in July 1216.

 # THE BARONS

King John's barons could rightly count themselves among the most powerful men in England – they had great wealth and owned lands that could take days to cross on horseback. John's attitude, however, was that his barons owned nothing except that which he granted to them or property that he allowed them to retain. The king, after all, ruled by the grace of God and with the blessing of the pope (most of the time, that is; John fell out with the pope just as he did with many other allies). This gave the king absolute power – and that's what really drove the barons to the point of war.

There were 25 barons, each of whom is mentioned in detail elsewhere in this book, who were party to Magna Carta and present for the negotiations at Runnymede. These were men who, for the most part, were masters of their own territories. They each held various castles, presided over their own courts and administered justice according to the law. They were familiar with legal documents and would have issued their own charters to resolve issues or settle disputes on their own estates. In short, each baron understood the magnitude of the demands that were presented to King John on 10 June 1215.

The conference at Runnymede was not the first time that King John had met with representatives of his "rebel" barons. They had presented their grievances to the king at court on his return, in late 1214, from his disastrous campaign to recapture his lands in Normandy. By January 1215, the rebels were fortifying their castles, gathering their forces and preparing for war. The barons agreed to meet with King John at the Temple Church in London. The king was under the protection of the powerful and wealthy order of the Knights Templar and had no hesitation in rejecting the barons' demands that he restore their ancient rights under the Charter of Liberties – also known as the Coronation Charter – issued by King Henry I when he came to the throne in 1100.

What the barons wanted was protection under the law for their property, lands and titles. It was all too easy for King John to abuse his powers by imposing taxes and fines on his subjects whenever he needed to raise money. Consequently, some noblemen found themselves in huge debt from the time they inherited their estates and the debts of their fathers, until the day they died. The way that the king could decide to revoke their titles and either seize their estates or award them to someone else had become intolerable.

Attempts by the Church to mediate between the barons and the king – and there is some evidence to suggest that it may have been Stephen Langton, Archbishop of Canterbury, who proposed that the barons use the Charter of Liberties as a bargaining tool – floundered. The barons renounced their vows of allegiance to King John and, in May, John ordered his officials to take control of the castles and lands of his enemies. Civil war was erupting and hostilities broke out all over the country.

Not all of John's barons sided with the rebels, and not all of them stayed staunchly loyal to the king. Some chose to sit on the fence, waiting to see which way the tide of war would turn. On 17 May, it turned against King John when the barons captured London. With his capital in enemy hands, the king was forced back to the negotiating table, this time at Runnymede.

Although many of the baron's demands were intended purely to secure their own positions, they also proposed sweeping reforms, which, in guaranteeing King John's adherence to the terms of the charter, significantly diminished his power as sovereign.

The "security clause" in Magna Carta essentially hands the reins of power to the barons (*see Clause 61, page 154*).

This clause not only gave the barons the right to rally their forces and wage war on the king whenever he stepped out of line, but also compelled the king's subjects to swear loyalty to the barons. It established rule by government, the government being the 25 barons, rather than absolute rule by the monarch. Thus the king was made answerable to the barons for any misdemeanours. King John would remain on the throne but would no longer have the traditional power of a monarch.

The barons intended Magna Carta as a peace formula and were willing to re-swear their fealty to King John, which they duly did when he agreed to their terms. To maintain stability, they needed to have a king as head of state. Overthrowing John was not an ideal option because they had no one with a strong enough claim to the throne to replace him. Getting rid of John would certainly have led to protracted disputes over who had a recognized legal right to the throne.

When John eventually sought support from the pope to have Magna Carta thrown out, the barons turned to Prince Louis, son of the French King Philip II. Most of the barons, it should be noted, were descended from the Norman knights who had invaded England with William the Conqueror in 1066, and still had strong connections with the French. Louis had married the granddaughter of King Henry II (King John's father), so he had some connection to the throne of England. More importantly, he could bring a strong military force across the Channel.

The war that became known as The First Barons' War saw many of John's supporters change sides to support the rebels and Prince Louis, but when John died in 1216, it became clear that the barons could achieve all of their aims by supporting the right of John's nine-year-old son, Henry, to take the throne. The boy would surely be easier to control than his father.

In September 1217, after the majority of the rebel barons defected from his side to support young King Henry III, Prince Louis signed The Treaty of Lambeth. Magna Carta formed part of that peace agreement. The barons could now return to their estates and concentrate on rebuilding England, setting war aside, at least for a while.

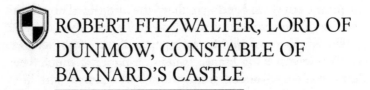 ## ROBERT FITZWALTER, LORD OF DUNMOW, CONSTABLE OF BAYNARD'S CASTLE

"Marshal of the Army of God" was how Robert FitzWalter styled himself when his fellow barons chose him as their leader in the struggle against King John. This did not mean to say that the barons wanted to install him on the throne in place of John – and nor did FitzWalter himself want that. When they embarked on their war against the king, the barons, in fact, did not want to replace John at all. Removing the king from power would only lead to a long war as various claimants to the throne emerged and the entire country was reduced to factional fighting.

What the barons wanted was for King John to recognize the Coronation Charter and the rights that it gave them. Their list of demands in The Articles of the Barons' document, to which King John eventually attached his seal

– with FitzWalter leading those negotiations at Runnymede – was the blueprint for Magna Carta. When that agreement was reached, there was no king in waiting, ready to step into John's shoes.

When King John backed out of the deal, it was clear that he would have to be replaced, but the barons wisely decided on an outsider to become king. FitzWalter and his close comrade Saer de Quincy made for France to entreat Prince Louis, son of the French King Philip II to step into his shoes.

Like most English barons, FitzWalter had strong ties in France. It was to France that he had fled when his relationship with King John hit an all-time low in 1212. John suspected some of his barons of plotting against him after the pope ostensibly released them from their obligations to John during the king's conflict with the pope. To secure their good behaviour, the king ordered each baron to send a blood relative to him as a hostage. Rather than comply, FitzWalter made for France, where he remained until King John resolved his differences with the pope and he was able to return safely in 1213.

Prince Louis, therefore, was the barons' choice and FitzWalter led the barons in paying homage to him when he arrived in London in June 1216. FitzWalter remained loyal to Louis until the end of the uprising, swearing allegiance to King Henry III only after the barons were defeated.

FitzWalter went on to serve the new king. He embarked on the Fifth Crusade in 1219, taking part in the siege of Damietta in Egypt. Fitzwalter died in December 1235, aged around 55.

 LONDON

Although London had existed as a major population centre for a thousand years before the time of Magna Carta, it had seen its fortunes and its population wax and wane over the centuries. The city was thriving once again when the Normans arrived in 1066, and William the Conqueror was crowned king in an elaborate ceremony in the newly completed Westminster Abbey on Christmas Day that year.

Westminster, however, was not London. Today, London is often described as a series of small towns or villages that have grown together. Wimbledon Village, to the southwest of the city, is as much a part of London as Hampstead Village, to the north, and the idea of a major city being a series of villages can apply to every modern conurbation. At the beginning of the thirteenth century, however, London was a distinct town on the banks of the Thames and scattered round about there really were a series of separate villages. That began to change during the Norman era.

King William immediately began work on fortifying the area. London was the largest city in England and the major trading port. His plan was to encircle the area with a series of castles that were about a day's march from London and from each other. This would allow them to reinforce each other quickly if required, but also provided for ease of communication. A day's march – around 20 miles (32 km) – for a column of armed men was little more than an hour's ride for a messenger on a fast horse. William started with a castle in the southeast corner of the city. Expanded and further fortified by later monarchs, this first castle became the Tower of London. For William, it was a royal residence and his treasury. Previously, Winchester was the Saxon capital of

England and the place where the treasury had traditionally been housed. However, once the Tower of London was used as a royal mint, it made sense for it also to become the treasury and the British Crown Jewels are kept there to this day.

By 1097, William II had begun work close to the abbey on Westminster Hall and the beginnings of the Palace of Westminster, which was to become the new royal residence and, ultimately, the seat of government (more commonly known as the Houses of Parliament). As many of the affairs of government became more centralized, the royal court started to rest more often in one place instead of constantly touring the country and the City of Westminster came to be regarded as the capital of England. The distinction between Westminster and London was not, however, to last for very long.

Westminster was another of London's "villages" but Norman builders had already begun to link the bustling city and port area of London with the area surrounding the abbey upriver to the west. Great stone mansions that were home to barons, bishops and the wealthiest merchants were built along what is now London's Strand. The River Thames flowing through London was at that time wider and shallower than it is now, a tidal river with natural river banks rather than the stone and concrete embankments that constrict it today. "Strand" is an old word for "shore" or "beach" and, when the tide was in, the new houses became waterfront properties. Its proximity to Westminster made this a desirable area for the rich and powerful, but there were other advantages to living west of the main city of London.

The prevailing wind in England tends to come from the west or southwest, so building a grand house to the west of the city meant that the smoke and smell of the city was blown away from a home rather than towards it. And the city would certainly not have smelt sweet. With an estimated 80,000 people living in London in the early years of the thirteenth century, there would have been quite a stench, especially on hot days. There was no proper sanitation, so household waste was simply thrown into the nearest stream or into a pile near the house. There were lots of small rivers and streams running through and around London, all of which have now been covered over and incorporated into the sewer system, draining from the rolling hills to the north of the city. While these helped to flush waste down into the Thames and out to sea, it wouldn't have taken much to clog them up – the Thames is a tidal waterway, so when the tide was coming in, the waste wasn't likely to go far. Add to that the fact that cooking was done over open fires, and one can imagine the cloud of smoke that hung over the city.

Despite all of that, London was an exciting place to be. Substantial new stone buildings were appearing on a regular basis; ships jostled for space on the quays in the port area and markets flourished all round the city. In addition to the wool, grain, wine and other trade goods that flooded into the city, almost everything else had to be imported – from firewood to building materials and food. Households might have space to keep a few chickens or rabbits, but urban living was different to the rural lifestyle and there wasn't room for livestock. There was a livestock market at Smithfield, which is still the city's meat market today.

The most densely populated areas of London were a maze of twisting streets and the buildings were mainly timber-framed, wattle-and-daub constructions. As well as being unsanitary, they posed a fire hazard – despite a ruling that all houses should have slate roofs, many were built using thatch. The fire hazard would be realized in 1666, when much of the city burned down.

The countryside, however, wasn't really that far away. London was surrounded by fields, meadows and woodland

and people in the surrounding villages supplied goods to the markets in London. The open space also meant that there was room for wealthy young men and squires to stage horse races or impromptu tournaments. As well as being a centre for transport (the Normans built the first stone bridge across the Thames in 1176), London had a huge military presence. One of its most elite groups was the Knights Templar. These were "Soldiers of God", the Order of Solomon's Temple, who had become an enormously wealthy and powerful institution all over Europe during the Crusades. Their English headquarters were based around Temple Church. It was here that King John agreed to meet with representatives of the barons in 1215, knowing that he was safe under the protection of the Knights Templar and believing that he had the people of London behind him.

 EUSTACE DE VESCI, LORD OF ALNWICK

The Lord of Alnwick Castle in Northumberland, Eustace de Vesci was 45 years old and a seasoned soldier at the time of the barons' revolt. A member of a group often referred to as the "northern barons", Vesci was married to Margaret, the illegitimate daughter of William the Lion, King of Scotland.

Vesci was a loyal lieutenant of King Richard I, serving with him on crusade and in Anjou, which may explain why he wasn't quite such an enthusiastic supporter of King John. Nevertheless, he did accompany King John on campaign in Ireland in 1210, but was accused of plotting to assassinate the king in 1212. He fled north to Scotland.

Although Vesci was later allowed to return to his estates, King John ordered that his castles at Alnwick and Malton in

North Yorkshire should be destroyed. However, the castles survived – as did the enmity between the two men. This bad feeling was, doubtless, further fuelled by stories that King John had attempted to seduce Vesci's wife.

When the king called for support for his military adventures in France, Vesci refused to take part or pay scutage. And when the barons began organizing themselves against the king, Vesci and his Yorkshire relative Robert de Ros were quick to join in.

Eustace de Vesci chose to side with Prince Louis of France in the chaotic civil war that followed the king's rejection of Magna Carta. He was heading south, escorting his brother-in-law, King Alexander II of Scotland, to pay homage to Louis, when he became involved in the siege of Barnard Castle in County Durham. Venturing too close to the castle walls, Vesci was shot in the head by an arrow and killed.

WILLIAM DE MOWBRAY, LORD OF AXHOLME

If anyone had good reason to hold a grievance against King John, it was surely William de Mowbray. He held lands across Yorkshire and Lincolnshire, including the Isle of Axholme and also land in Surrey, some of which had been granted to the Mowbray family by King Henry I, a century before.

A hundred years or so is nothing, however, when it comes to family feuds over disputed land and Mowbray found an old quarrel raising its head again in 1200. The man spoiling for a fight was William de Stuteville, Sheriff of Lincolnshire, whose ancestor, Robert de Stuteville, had supported Robert Curthose (the brother of King Henry I) in his attempt to take the English throne from Henry. When the attempt failed, Henry confiscated some of the Stuteville lands and gave them to the Mowbrays. The Stutevilles had been agitating for the return of their lands ever since.

Mowbray agreed to pay King John the enormous sum of 2000 marks to settle the dispute. Stuteville, however, was a loyal vassal of the king and John's solution was a compromise, with Mowbray handing over a large tract of the disputed territory, as well as paying the hefty bill.

It is unsurprising, therefore, that Mowbray joined the rebel barons against John after the king threw out Magna Carta. Although short in stature (he was said to be as small as a dwarf), Mowbray was renowned for his bravery and was taken prisoner while fighting at the Battle of Lincoln in 1217.

While ordinary prisoners were generally executed as a matter of course, noblemen were usually held to ransom and Mowbray was forced to sign over his estate at Banstead in Surrey to secure his release. He died at Axholme around 1224, probably aged about 50.

 # WINDSOR

Queen Elizabeth II spent much of her formative years at Windsor. The Royal Lodge in Windsor Great Park was home to her parents, the Duke and Duchess of York, before the abdication of Edward VIII, the duke's brother, thrust him into the limelight as King George VI. There is still a miniature cottage – a scale playhouse – in the grounds of the lodge that was given to Elizabeth by the people of Wales when she was a young girl.

During the Second World War, the young Princess Elizabeth and her sister, Princess Margaret Rose, were evacuated to

Windsor to escape the danger of bombing raids on London. When she became Queen Elizabeth in 1952, Windsor Castle became her favourite weekend retreat from the noise and bustle of London.

The British royal family's association with Windsor in the twentieth century could not be closer. During the First World War, the family – who belonged to the German House of Saxe-Coburg and Gotha – decided that it would be a good PR move to change their name to something a little less Germanic and opted to name themselves after their favourite castle. They became the House of Windsor in 1917.

The history of Windsor Castle and its connection with the royal household does, of course, stretch back much further than the beginning of the twentieth century. It is the oldest, and largest, occupied castle in the world, having been inhabited continuously over a period of almost 1,000 years.

It was the Norman invader William the Conqueror who first turned the castle into a major fortification in the 1070s. His strategic plan was to build a ring of motte-and-bailey castles about a day's march from London and each within a day's march – about 20 miles (32 km) – of the next. Windsor was among the most important because it protected the western approaches via the River Thames, travelling by boat on a river being the fastest way to get around at that time. Queen Elizabeth can be whisked by limousine from Buckingham Palace in central London to Windsor Castle with a police escort in less than an hour, but that wasn't an option for William the Conqueror!

William's castle at Windsor was basically a wooden keep built on a man-made mound (the motte) on a rocky outcrop sitting about 100 feet (30 metres) above the River Thames. More wooden structures were added as the years went by, and stone was gradually used to replace the wood. In 1154, when King John's father, Henry II, became king, he undertook extensive rebuilding in stone, turning the castle into a mighty fortress.

By the time of Magna Carta in 1215, King John had also undertaken work at Windsor Castle. This was mainly to improve the royal quarters rather than the fortifications, which were sorely tested when the rebel barons besieged the castle in 1214. The following year, Windsor Castle became King John's base in June, when he spent the best part of a week travelling to and from Runnymede during the Magna Carta negotiations. Another year on and Windsor Castle was under siege yet again, with the barons – supported by Prince Louis' French troops – failing to breech its defences.

From the time when it stood witness to the historic Magna Carta, the castle continued to grow in size and became a favourite royal residence – which it remains to this day.

 # LADY NICHOLAA DE LA HAYE

One of King John's staunchest supporters throughout the troubles with his rebellious barons was Lady Nicholaa de la Haye. She was around the same age as John, but must have reminded him very much of his own mother when he met her in Lincoln during the war in 1216. She had successfully held Lincoln Castle for the Crown against a superior force that had occupied the city, led by Gilbert de Gant. Nicholaa, a fabulously wealthy woman, had cleverly negotiated a truce by buying her way out of trouble.

Born around 1156, Nicholaa was the eldest daughter of Richard de la Haye and inherited his extensive estates in Lincolnshire, including the right to hold the office of Castellan of Lincoln. She married twice, but remained very much in control of her property. Her second husband, Gerard de Camville, was apparently more than happy to leave his wife in charge of Lincoln in 1191, while he fought alongside the then Prince John to capture castles at Nottingham and Tickhill during John's attempt to usurp his brother, Richard I, while he was away on crusade. At that time, Nicholaa held out for more than a month against mercenary soldiers intent on sacking the town.

Although both Gerard and Nicholaa were very much out of favour with King Richard when he briefly returned to England, they were able to use their great wealth to buy forgiveness. Gerard died early in 1215, but Nicholaa, having remained loyal to King John, remained in charge of her estates. She was made joint Sheriff of Lincoln by John (along with the king's man Philip Mark) when he must have been close to being on his deathbed.

Nicholaa supported John's son, Henry III, when he came to the throne. She defended Lincoln against her enemies many more times before she finally retired to a manor house in Swaton in Lincolnshire in 1226, where she died four years later.

 RICHARD DE PERCY, 5TH BARON PERCY

Another baron who was often referred to as one of the "northern lords", Richard de Percy was the son of Agnes, the great granddaughter of William de Percy.

William was a Norman nobleman who had arrived in England around the time of the invasion in 1066. By 1086, the Domesday Book recorded that he held 118 manors in Lincolnshire, Yorkshire, Essex and Hampshire. Agnes was heiress to the Percy family estates and when she married

Joscelin de Louvain, he changed his name in order to perpetuate the Percy line. Richard was their second son, his older brother having died in 1198. He inherited half of the family lands when his mother died around 1203.

Like other northern lords, Percy served King John in a military capacity up until 1214 when the king demanded support for his expedition to France. Percy declined to participate: the following year he was fighting alongside the rebel barons against the king.

One of the barons selected to be excommunicated by the pope for rising up against King John, Percy supported the French Prince Louis' claim to the English throne but did not immediately decide to switch sides when King John died. It was not until November 1217 that Percy gave up the fight, finally accepting Henry III as king.

Percy died some time in 1244, probably in his mid-sixties. He had married twice but never had children. His nephew inherited his estates and the Percy family went on to become a historic force in British history, surviving to this day as the Dukes of Northumberland.

 # BOYS AND MEN

Not so long ago, it was widely assumed that the concept of "childhood" simply didn't exist in the Middle Ages. The view was that the kind of life led by a modern child – where good health, play and education experienced as part of a loving family environment is seen as the norm – was in stark contrast to the lives of children 800 years ago, who were treated as a burden to be tolerated until they were old enough to be of some use.

Recent research, however, shows that this may not have been entirely the case. Studies of toys from the period have shown that children were encouraged to play. The toys may have been homemade in many cases, but models of mounted knights made out of metal would have been bought or specially commissioned, showing that some parents cared enough about their children's play time to lavish gifts on them.

Children do not feature prominently in illustrated manuscripts, paintings or tapestries doing anything more than emulating their parents, but in some cases they can be seen playing games like tag or "king of the castle" and riding on hobby-horses. They were, it seems, encouraged to play and enjoy an active childhood, although their lives were set on a predetermined course at an early age.

In the early thirteenth century, a child surviving the first year of life had a reasonable chance of fighting off disease long enough to acquire the strength needed to survive in the harsh and unhygienic medieval world. In fact, 25 per cent of those born to wealthy parents and up to 50 per cent of those born to the poor did not. A whole host of infectious diseases for which we now have myriad names would then simply have been classed as "fever" or "food poisoning". Life expectancy was only around 30 years, although anyone from the ruling classes who made it, strong and healthy, to the age of 21, might well have had another 40 years to look forward to. In the fourteenth century, the Black Death was to reduce life expectancy dramatically.

In the days of King John, however, a fit young boy born into a noble family could expect to live in his parents' grand house or castle until he was about seven years old. He would then be sent off to live in another castle, most likely in the house of a nobleman a rung or two up the feudal ladder from his own parents, perhaps even in one of the king's own residences.

Here he would serve first as a page, running errands and generally waiting on the lords and ladies of the household. However, he would also learn how a large house functioned and how people interacted with one another, as well as learning about customs and proper manners. He might also be taught how to read and understand Latin and, if it were not already his native tongue, the version of French spoken by the Norman nobility.

A young boy would also learn how to ride and, if he showed promise, he might, when he was around 14 years old, become apprenticed to a knight as a squire. They had to train hard to learn the art of combat, which included lifting heavy stones to build muscle, throwing the javelin, fighting with a quarterstaff, archery, wrestling, acrobatics and sword fighting. Swordsmanship was taught using a blunted sword and a buckler, a small shield the size of a pot lid. This trained the would-be knight how to parry sword thrusts and how to use his shield as an offensive weapon without the novice having to start off with a full-sized, cumbersome shield. Similarly, the blunted sword was used against heavily padded protective layers, although the dull blade could still inflict painful wounds.

The squire would learn how to clean and prepare the knight's armour and weapons, although major repairs had to be undertaken by a blacksmith or armourer. He would also need to help his knight put on his armour, which meant more than simply helping him to dress – the various elements of the heavy steel all had to be strapped into place in the correct sequence to make sure that they overlapped and allowed for movement in the right way.

This, of course, meant that the squire went with his knight to compete in tournaments. He would eventually get the chance to compete in his own right, even before he became a knight, as there were special contests organized solely for squires.

Whether a squire lived in his knight's house, or whether he lived in a baron's castle where landless knights also lived as part of the baron's permanent military force, he would have regular chores to perform, which would include acting as a servant when his masters sat down to eat. Squires were expected, for example, to learn the correct way to carve meat at the table.

The squire's apprenticeship would last until he was around 21 years of age, at which point he might expect to be knighted himself. However, he might want to avoid that happening – a squire could be made a knight either by his local lord or by the king, but it wasn't an honour that everyone could afford. The squire's family, whom he may have visited only a couple of times a year since he was sent away as a seven-year-old, would have to pay for the costly armour, weapons and warhorse that a knight required, as well as funding any forays he might make to tournaments far and wide. Being a knight could be prohibitively expensive, especially if a second, third or fourth son, who might not inherit any part of his father's estate when he died (the bulk of property often being bequeathed to the first-born).

Around the beginning of the thirteenth century, there was a growing "middle class" of merchants, tradesmen and professionals, particularly in the new cities and busy ports. Trade with continental Europe had expanded enormously since the Norman Conquest, although Anglo-Saxon entrepreneurs are known to have traded extensively with partners as far away as Russia. Clauses 41 and 42 of Magna Carta make special mention of such merchants.

The son of a merchant would live an entirely different life from that of a boy born into the nobility. From a very young age, he would learn about the family business, in order to play a full part as soon as he was old enough. A boy might also become apprenticed to another merchant or tradesman, a privilege for which his family would have to pay, and be sent away from home to live with his new master.

Merchants, especially those dealing in foreign trade, had to be able to speak and read Latin, which was the international language of commerce, the legal profession and the Church. The sons of the middle classes learned Latin either through private tuition or at one of the new schools that were beginning to appear.

Merchants donated money to set up schools in the most important trading towns and boys would be sent to school to learn arithmetic and Latin grammar, the institutions becoming known as grammar schools. The schools were allied to a particular trade, making them private schools, although fee-paying schools would later be established that were open to anyone who could pay, such establishments being termed "public" schools.

There would have been few if any books in schools. These were hugely expensive, hand-written items – the first printed books didn't begin appearing until the mid-fifteenth century. Boys learned their lessons verbally, repeating their Latin phrases time and time again, and earning themselves a beating if they got anything wrong.

Some might learn mathematics or become proficient in the use of an abacus, but few would continue their formal education beyond a basic level or contemplate attending one of the new universities.

As the oldest university in the English-speaking world, Oxford University had been growing in stature since the latter part of the eleventh century and the colleges of Cambridge University can trace their history back to around the same time.

Peasants, still by far and away the largest portion of the population, could not afford to send their sons to school. A peasant boy was expected to do chores as soon as he was old enough to learn how to feed chickens or help to herd livestock. When he was strong enough, he would help with the back-breaking work in the fields and perhaps spend some time working in the local landowner's house or castle, if such was required by the terms of his family's tenure.

The Church played a major role in everyone's lives and even the most lowly peasants attended church on a regular basis. However, all services were conducted in Latin, so most people couldn't understand what was being said – sometimes not even the priest. Despite being the most educated man in the village, while the priest might be able to pronounce written Latin, the chances are he did not understand it. For a lucky few, a well-educated priest might teach boys how to read, but even as late as the fourteenth century it has been estimated that 8 out of 10 adults in England were unable even to spell their own names.

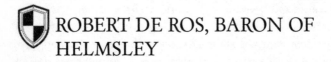 ROBERT DE ROS, BARON OF HELMSLEY

One of the 25 barons appointed to ensure that King John adhered to the terms of Magna Carta, Robert de Ros was connected to Eustace de Vesci insofar as both men had married illegitimate daughters of William the Lion, King of Scotland (Ros's wife was Isabella). Ros, however, had previously enjoyed a far better relationship with the king than Vesci ever had.

Unlike Vesci, Ros had not been a particular favourite of King Richard I, who had ordered him to be arrested and imprisoned in 1197. When Ros escaped, his former jailor was hanged. Ros was more of a supporter of King John, yet he had problems with this king as well. At various times King

John ordered Ros's lands to be seized then reinstated. After Ros became a monk, he gave his lands to another, but later appointed him Sheriff of Cumberland.

Ros may have supported the rebel barons, but, unlike Vesci, he did not show his hand from the very beginning, perhaps in order to try to hold on to the property that kept slipping through his fingers. By the time the barons mustered their forces at Stamford, however, Ros was on the side of the rebels.

After the death of King John and the withdrawal of Prince Louis, Ros pledged allegiance to the young King Henry III. Ten years later, Ros was back in the monastery again, where he died in 1227, at the age of 45. He was buried in the Temple Church in London.

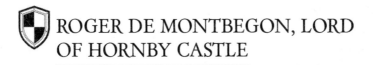 ROGER DE MONTBEGON, LORD OF HORNBY CASTLE

With estates in Lancashire, Nottinghamshire, Lincolnshire and Yorkshire, Roger de Montbegon was one of four barons who had refused to take any part in King John's campaign in France in 1214. The others were fellow northerners Eustace de Vesci, William de Mowbray and Richard de Percy. These men were close allies, Montbegon even acting as guarantor for debts that Vesci and Mowbray owed to the king.

Yet Montbegon had once been an ally of King John. He had supported John in his move against his mother, when she held the English throne for John's older brother, King Richard I, while he was being held to ransom in Germany. John's attempt to take the throne failed and Richard punished Montbegon by taking some of his estates. Eventually, his land was returned to him and Montbegon must have been very pleased when Richard died and John became king.

In 1199, King John held the marriage rights to Olivia, widow of Robert Fitzjohn, and Montbegon asked to take her as his bride. John agreed, for the regal sum of 500 marks. Montbegon, it seemed, was not such a favourite of John's as he might have thought.

John's seeming ingratitude for past services, on top of Montbegon's grievances concerning taxes and land seizures, was certainly enough to persuade the baron to throw in his lot with the rebels. For three years after the war was over, Montbegon was embroiled in fighting to recover lost land and, even though he had been one of the 25 barons tasked with ensuring Magna Carta was obeyed, he fell foul of the law by rejecting decisions of the courts and taking by force property that he felt was his. Montbegon died in his early sixties, in 1226.

 THE KNIGHTS

When William, Duke of Normandy, landed his invasion force at Pevensey in Sussex, towards the end of September in 1066, the number of men who actually came ashore has been estimated at anything from a paltry 7,500 to a hugely ambitious 150,000. Shipping anything like 150,000 men across the English Channel would have been a near impossible logistical feat at the time and it is likely that William's army was less than 10 per cent of that size. What is known is that he brought with him a substantial number of horses – around a quarter of his troops were cavalry.

The Norman knights were a formidable mounted force, but could only be properly deployed under the right circumstances. The English King Harold's troops, weary from a long march south, after defeating Norwegian invaders at Stamford Bridge in Yorkshire, had a substantial territorial advantage with their ranks formed at the top of a ridge. William's infantry were repelled but, when Harold's men broke ranks to chase the fleeing invaders, the Norman knights thundered in on their warhorses, catching the English infantry in the open and cutting them to pieces.

Knights were highly trained, highly skilled horsemen and warriors. They spent years learning to use a sword and how to fight with knives, axes, maces, hammers and all manner of weapons, before learning how to do it all over again on horseback. Knights were elite troops, either on foot or mounted, and the impressive sight of a knight in battle armour was enough to send a thrill of fear through any humble foot soldier.

Prior to the arrival of these fearsome cavalrymen from northern Europe, fighting on horseback was not such a common occurrence in England. Horses were symbols of wealth, both expensive to buy and to maintain. A nobleman who rode off to battle was likely to do just that: ride to the battle and leave his expensive horse safely on the sidelines, while he waded into the fray on foot.

Knights were soldiers, first and foremost, but their training, weapons, armour and horses came at a great cost, making attaining the rank of "knight" something to which only those with money could aspire. Once he was knighted, a young man might still have no real source of income. Some of the wealthiest landowners might house a squadron of knights in their castles (for their own protection and to enforce their rule), but by the time of Magna Carta, a knight was more likely to hold lands himself, either from a more senior knight, a baron, or from the king. A knight was, therefore, likely to have responsibilities under the feudal system and to be lord of his own manor rather than simply a garrison soldier or a mercenary.

As well as being schooled in martial arts, however, a knight was also taught the "code of chivalry", made up of unwritten rules that were supposed to dictate the way a knight conducted himself both on and off the field of battle. Knights, no matter how ferocious they were in combat, were expected to behave in a courteous manner at other times, especially in the presence of ladies. Heroic poems such as *The Song of Roland*, composed in the late eleventh century, and known to have been very popular around the time of Magna Carta, describe the ideals of chivalry, maintaining that a knight should:

Fear God and maintain His Church
Serve your liege lord with valour and loyalty
Protect the weak and defenceless
Show compassion to widows and orphans
Refrain from being crude or offensive
Live by honour and for glory
Do not act purely for financial gain
Fight for the welfare of all
Obey those placed in authority
Guard the honour of fellow knights
Avoid unfairness, meanness and deceit
Keep faith
Never tell lies
Keep going until you complete a task
Respect the honour of women
Never refuse a challenge from an equal
Never turn your back on an enemy.

Some knights would even have taken vows along these lines but, while the idea of being courteous undoubtedly made life less fraught in social situations, when it came to a fight, the rules were often left behind with the ladies. Politeness and unbridled aggression seldom share the same space for any length of time.

One of the places where knights could hone their fighting skills (when there was no actual war to fight) was at a tournament. The romantic connotation is two knights "jousting" in the lists, tilting at each other with lances, the aim being to knock an opponent off his horse but not necessarily to kill him. In fact, the first tournaments took place between groups of knights who fought pitched battles that could go on for hours. A cynical knight with an eye for a profit would hold off until the others were all but exhausted and then wade into the fray, a fresh horse and unwearied arms giving a tired and weak victim little chance. Having defeated his opponent – whether he survived the contest or not – the winner relieved him of his armour, his weapons, his horse and any other valuables or money he might have. The vanquished knight himself might even be held to ransom.

Tournaments could be an expensive business for the losers and their families, but highly profitable for the victors. These contests did, eventually, develop into slightly more civilized affairs, with rules and prize money, making the knights Europe's first international, professional sportsmen.

In England, having become landowners and administrators, as well as simply cavalry soldiers, knights were trusted to carry out special tasks thoroughly and honestly, as witnessed by Clause 48 of Magna Carta:

All evil customs relating to forests and warrens, foresters, warreners, sheriffs and their servants, or river-banks and their wardens, are at once to be investigated in every county by twelve sworn knights of the county, and within forty days of their enquiry the evil customs are to be abolished completely and irrevocably. But we, or our chief justice if we are not in England, are first to be informed.

Teams of knights, it would seem, were tasked with investigating the affairs of the forests and their reports most probably formed the basis for the Charter of the Forests in 1217.

Knights who performed well could rise to high office, as did William Marshal, who began fighting for honour and profit (the two were not always seen as incompatible) in tournaments. William was a younger son of a minor aristocrat, standing to inherit nothing when his father died, so he was forced to make his own way in the world after his father sent him to learn the arts of chivalry and knighthood at the home of a relative in France.

As a young knight, William became a favourite of Eleanor of Aquitaine when he fought in her name and was appointed by Henry II to instruct Henry the Young King. He also served King Richard I, King John and Henry III, and earned his rewards in the form of estates and titles, becoming Earl of Pembroke, Marshal of England. From starting out with neither lands nor titles, William Marshal used his skill as a knight to become one of the richest and most powerful men in England.

 # JOAN, LADY OF WALES

There were a number of remarkable women who played a part in the life of King John and influenced events around the time of Magna Carta, not least Joan, his illegitimate daughter. She was born in Normandy sometime around 1191 as a result of one of John's many sexual dalliances, in this instance with a woman called Clemence. Joan was brought to England by her father in 1203.

In order to try to build an alliance in the west with the problematic Welsh, John married Joan to Llewelyn the Great, the Prince of North Wales. Llewelyn had already agreed treaties with John by the time that he and Joan were married in 1205, but having Joan in Wales gave John a blood-relation ally to help ward off trouble from that quarter.

The marriage, it seems, was a success and the couple had at least two children together, Ellen and Dafydd. Llewelyn also highly rated his wife as a diplomat and she is known to have been heavily involved in smoothing relations between her father and her husband during their many confrontations.

Despite Joan's efforts, John was ready to wage war on the Welsh in 1212 and executed some of the Welsh hostages he held. However, Joan had heard of a potential rebellion by some of John's baron's and warned her father in time to stop him from committing his forces.

Joan played the same diplomatic role when her half-brother, Henry, came to the throne. She gained such respect that she even managed to secure a decree from the pope, declaring her a legitimate daughter of John. Although it stopped short of granting Joan any claim to the English throne, it did put her son, Dafydd, in a better position to inherit his father's title.

Welsh society was scandalized when Joan was discovered having an affair, in 1230. Llewelyn had her lover hanged and confined his wife to house arrest. Eventually, however, he seems to have forgiven her and when she died established the Friary of Llanfaes in Anglesey, dedicating it in her memory.

WILLIAM DE FORZ, COUNT OF AUMALE

William de Forz was a relative newcomer to the ranks of the nobility in England, his Norman title of Count of Aumale came from his mother's line. His English holdings also came from his mother, Countess Hawise, and included estates in Yorkshire, Cumberland and Lincolnshire, including Castle Bytham. If there is an example of a baron, motivated by an overriding concern for his own wealth and wellbeing, it is William. His attitude is also an indication of the political uncertainty of the time.

Forz arrived in England in 1214, marrying the daughter of Richard de Montfichet as a way of ensuring possession of his inheritance and retaining control of his property. Becoming a part of such an influential, aristocratic family brought him social status and powerful allies to discouarage anyone else who might want to lay claim to the estates his mother had left him. He was probably motivated to join the rebels in early 1215 in order to show solidarity with his father-in-law, as well as with his fellow barons.

Within a few months, however, he had decided to side with King John but Forz rejoined the rebels shortly before John's death. His support for John was probably given in return for the grant of more land and property, Forz acquiring a number of new estates during the course of the war – although he was forced to return these once the barons paid homage to Henry III.

Forz switched allegiance to the young king, after John's death, but he was not keen to comply with the demand that he give up his new lands. By 1220, despite being one of the 25 guarantors of Magna Carta, he was behaving like a rebel once again, using force of arms to fight for what he believed to be his. He was eventually accepted back into the royal fold, fighting for King Henry in France in 1230.

Forz had his last adventure in his late forties. He embarked on crusade in 1241, although he died on the way.

 JOHN DE LACY, CONSTABLE OF CHESTER

The eldest son of Roger de Lacy, John inherited his father's lands and titles when he reached his 21st birthday in 1213. Roger de Lacy had gone on the Third Crusade with Richard I and had fought for King John, holding Chateau Gaillard in Normandy through an eight-month siege in 1204, before being forced to surrender.

Roger de Lacy died in 1211 and in order to take control of his inheritance his son was forced to pay King John a huge fee. He also had to accept responsibility for any debts his father had owed to the Crown and hand over at least two of his castles to the king, manned by the king's troops at Lacy's expense. If that were not enough he was also obliged to swear an oath to the effect that, should he default on payments or rebel against the king, all of his lands and property would be forfeited to the Crown. The payment was an incredible 7000 marks, due over a period of three years.

Lacy, therefore, had every reason to remain loyal to King John and also every reason to despise him. He joined the king on his expedition to France in 1214; while he was not one of the first to join the rebel barons, he did so once they took control of London in 1215. It is impossible to know the pressures men like Lacy were under during the rebellion, but it can be assumed that self-interest and self-preservation were the main motivations for Lacy to return to the king's camp in early 1216 and then to side with the rebels again shortly before the king's death. Along with several other rebel barons, he swore fealty to King Henry in August 1217.

Lacy embarked on crusade the following year and was gone for two years. On his return, he took up several important posts, including King's Justice in Lincoln and Lancashire. He died in 1240 at the age of 48.

 # GIRLS AND WOMEN

It is easy to believe girls and women were treated as completely subordinate to men in medieval society: in many ways, they were. They did not have the same rights or freedoms in law (even when they were extremely wealthy); they were generally not as well educated as the most scholarly men; they were expected to defer to their husbands, taking second place to them, no matter what their social standing; and a son inherited his father's property and titles, even if his sister was older than him. Yet, women were still able to exert their influence on everyday life whether they were of peasant stock, a member of the merchant class or the ruling aristocracy.

Girls born into peasant families spent their foremost years, much as their brothers did, playing with other village children until they were gradually able to take on more and more chores. They looked after younger siblings and generally worked to support the family.

There were definite lines of demarcation when it came to the kind of work that girls did and the work that their brothers were expected to do. Cooking was, for the most part, women's work, which may seem like sexual stereotyping to modern eyes, but it was obviously a job that was less physical than others and one that didn't require brute strength.

A man's work might include ploughing, hedging, fencing, ditching and clearing trees to create new fields. Women would do the planting, weeding, winnowing (separating the grain from the chaff) and would tend to the chickens and the cows. They also looked after younger children who were not yet able to fend for themselves.

Young girls were expected to do all of these jobs. As was the case with boys, work could also be found for them – whether paid or as part of the family's obligations to their feudal lord – at the local manor house or castle. Work there would involve scrubbing floors, scouring pots in the kitchen, sometimes serving at meals, and certainly fetching and carrying pitchers of water to lords and ladies in their bedchambers or solars.

Water was seldom clean enough to be fit for drinking on its own, but people did use it for washing. The link had yet to be made between disease and poor hygiene since there was no understanding of the role that bacteria play in spreading disease. However, people recognized – in the way that all animals did – that if something tasted bad, you didn't eat or drink it – and if it smelled bad, you stayed well away from it.

Although it was not common practice for people to wash as often, or as thoroughly, as most of us do today, they did clean themselves – and even used soap. References to the use of soap can be found from around the eleventh century and it appears to have been made from ash and lime mixed with oil and fat from beef or mutton. Soap-making was developing into a major industry in Bristol towards the end of the twelfth century.

A peasant family, however, would not be able to afford luxuries such as soap. One of a peasant girl's jobs would be to fetch water from a stream or a well. Necessary for cooking, the water would also be used by those who had been working in the fields all day to rinse off some of the accumulation of mud and muck. Their quick wash would not include bathing. That, of course, required a bath – another unaffordable, unnecessary luxury – and copious amounts of water, all of which would have to be lugged home from the well in buckets. Heating water for a bath would also have used up firewood, which was not always in plentiful supply.

One thirteenth-century writer recorded his disdain at foreign settlers, traders from Denmark, whose habit it was to bathe once a week, who combed their hair every day and who changed their clothes regularly. He suspected them of doing so in order to ingratiate themselves with young English women.

Even the oldest English women would have been young by modern standards, only in their twenties. Girls who survived infancy and avoided the many fatal diseases that swept the country from time to time, still had an average life expectancy of just 25 years – far lower than their brothers'. The main reason for this was the high rate of death in childbirth, undoubtedly largely due to infections caused by poor sanitation and bad hygiene.

A young woman in her early to mid-twenties was of prime childbearing age and it was around this age that most couples were married. Although the Church decreed that the minimum age at which a girl could be married was just 12, and 14 for a boy, such young marriages (and some even younger, despite what the Church said) happened when the children's parents arranged the weddings to suit their own financial or political ambitions. That was seldom an issue amongst the lower classes.

For a girl whose father was a merchant or a professional living in a city, life would be markedly different. A peasant girl had little chance of receiving any kind of formal education, but the daughter of a tradesman, especially if he had no son, could well be expected to follow in her father's footsteps. That might mean learning the business from her parents, or it might involve being apprenticed, just like a boy would have been, to another merchant.

Girls worked in the silk and wool industries as spinners and weavers but also in breweries and even in foundries. Like boys, they would serve a seven-year apprenticeship and they might well find themselves working for a woman – in the cities, it was not unknown for women to be running their own businesses and taking on girls as apprentices. At the time of Magna Carta, however, with most of the population still living in a rural environment, a girl had little hope of embarking on a business career. The exceptions were, perhaps, those of noble birth, although their business would involve running an estate rather than a commercial enterprise.

The daughter of a great lord in the top tier of society would be taught to read Latin and possibly French. Her tutor was likely either to be a teacher hired by her father or a local clergyman who relied on her father for a large portion of his income. She would also learn about music, singing and dancing, and would spend a great deal of time perfecting her embroidery techniques.

Once such a girl could read – taught largely by looking at Bible passages or a book of prayers – she might be lucky enough to read one of the new "romances". These were not love stories, but rather tales of heroic knights and their adventures, written as poetry. Love stories also existed, as did books about history, but the books themselves were not printed and bound as this book is. Instead, they were handwritten manuscript pages sewn together. Needless to say, such books, especially those "illuminated manuscripts" filled with lavish illustrations, were very expensive, although not quite as expensive as they are today. In 2005, a compendium of medieval poetry and bawdy jokes that was made in 1320 sold at auction for £1.7 million.

Being able to read was essential for a girl of noble birth because her duties when she was a grown woman would involve dealing with documents and letters. She would first become accustomed to those duties by watching her mother at work, but as soon as she was old enough, she might well be sent away to the house of a higher-ranking noble family, just like her brothers.

Sending their children away like this could be an astute move on the part of ambitious parents keen to have a son or daughter acknowledged by those a few rungs up the social ladder and perhaps earmarked as a suitable wedding match. On the other hand, the overlord might well demand that children be sent to him as his wards to work as well-bred servants and to act as unofficial hostages. Having a potential troublemaker's child and heir under your roof and at your mercy was one way to persuade a rebellious underling to behave.

Whether she was there by choice or by force, a young girl would became a handmaiden or lady-in-waiting to the noblewoman, and would watch and learn how a large house was run. The average day for the wife of a baron might begin with morning mass, probably a private ceremony in the castle chapel, followed by a quick breakfast and a round of briefings with servants to give them any special instructions for the day or to sort out any problems.

A lady would not be expected to deal with all of the castle staff but would meet with personal staff, the chief cook and the clerk of the kitchen or the steward who was in charge of the army of servants. She might then have to spend some time looking over the domestic accounts before having lunch at around midday.

If there were guests staying at the castle, the noblewoman

would need to ensure that they were being properly entertained, perhaps accompanying them on hunting or hawking trips. If her husband was away, then she was in sole charge not only of her household, but the whole estate. She would have to hold court, dealing with complaints and sitting in judgement on legal matters. And if the aforementioned rebellious troublemaker and his troops came charging over the hill, she would have to play the role of castellan, directing her soldiers in the defence of the castle.

Sometime during the course of the day, a noblewoman would check on her own children, ensuring that they were in lessons or in training alongside the children of any other nobles in her care. If she had a very young child, she would also talk to the wet nurse to make sure the baby was doing well. Normally, noblewomen did not breastfeed their own children but hired a local woman to do it – children were usually breastfed until they were around two years old.

This created a strong bond between a child and his or her nurse, so much so that, when the child grew to adulthood, the nurse might find herself being awarded a small house and a scrap of land in gratitude.

Not every wife would see herself as being competent to organize her defenders in a castle under siege, even if the stories of Eleanor of Aquitaine leading her own squadron of armour-clad Amazons into battle during the Second Crusade – stories that had shocked and delighted the gossip-loving aristocracy all over Europe – could be believed (which they couldn't). Some young ladies, however, grew to become noblewomen who knew how to look after themselves. Provisions were made in Magna Carta in Clause 8 to protect the rights of widows. This was for the very good reason that these women often fell prey to unscrupulous suitors who would kidnap and marry them in order to get their hands on inherited land and property.

Kidnapping, however, was not always necessary. A widow who inherited property that was held either from an overlord or directly from the king could be offered in marriage by her liege lord to one of his trusted cronies – this ensured that the land remained under his control, the power associated with the titles remained safe, borders stayed secure and the revenue stream continued to flow.

As far as the overlord or the king was concerned, if there were several suitable husbands in waiting, he might offer the widow to the highest bidder. When King John was considering just such a bid for Agnes de Hastings, the widow of Ralph of Cornhill, Agnes decided to bid for her own marriage rights, offering the king 200 marks, three horses and two hawks. She won.

 CLOTHING

The wife of a thirteenth-century nobleman in England would have been very much aware of the fashions of the time. Although the clothes worn by aristocratic ladies hadn't really changed a great deal over previous decades, fashion was starting to become something of an issue.

The basic dress or gown had started out as a kind of shapeless kaftan, tight around the neck and hanging to the floor. Gradually, changes were made with the addition of a belt or tie, called a girdle, to bring the gown in at the waist and give the outfit some shape. The neckline was worn lower, becoming square-cut, while sleeves varied in length and volume.

Once this shapeless garment had been given some form, it became more figure-hugging: a dress could be laced up the back or in front to make it easier to put on, although this also made it easy to draw the garment tight around the body. Elaborate decorative details were added to sleeves, neckline and bodice. By the time of Magna Carta, girdles were drifting in and out of fashion, as was the shape of the neckline, which could be cut lower to be more revealing. However, dresses were still long enough to sweep the floor.

The wealthy chose silk as a fabric. If not of silk, then a gown would be made from the finest woven wool, with a linen smock worn underneath for warmth and comfort, and woollen stockings gartered above the knee.

Leather shoes were held in place by a strap across the top of the foot. In the unlikely event that a lady should have to walk on soft, muddy or wet ground, wooden soles could be strapped onto the shoes to protect them.

A great lord dressed in a long tunic over which he wore a surcoat or supertunic. He wore breeches that reached to his knee, although these might not be visible as his tunic could reach down well below the knee. Long stockings were worn inside leather boots that could reach up to the thigh, although shorter boots and shoes were also fashionable, especially for wearing indoors. Boots were definitely required outdoors for riding.

Just as his lady enjoyed the finest quality wool and silk, so too did the lord. Sleeves that were slashed at the shoulder to reveal contrasting colours beneath became fashionable. The lord's tunic might be embroidered with his coat of arms or, again like his wife's gown, decorated with jewels or pearls. When he married Isabella of Angoulême, King John's outfit was said to be far more opulent than his bride's. He was certainly known for his love of collecting jewellery and gems.

For travelling, or for outdoors, heavy woollen cloaks were worn, trimmed or lined with fur for warmth. When such a cumbersome garment was not required, gentlemen also had the option to wear a scalloped shoulder cape that might also incorporate a hood – a kind of medieval hoodie. Linen skullcaps were also worn, with other, more stylish headgear worn on top.

Women wore make-up and perfume, using powder to achieve a pale complexion. At one point, they used powdered lead, but this seeped into the skin, causing painful skin complaints and, ultimately, madness from lead poisoning. Ground cuttlefish, flour or even lard were used. The idea was that a lady should have pale skin to reflect her status – only common women who laboured outdoors in the fields had suntanned skin.

Eyeshadow, eyeliner, mascara and lip rouge consisted of powders derived from soot, charcoal or berries. Ladies would use saliva to moisten the powders in order to apply them. In the thirteenth century, a more natural complexion also became popular and powders were coloured to accommodate this. Hair could be dyed, again using natural products, and curling irons were used to add some bounce. On a day-to-day basis, the hair was more likely to be worn gathered in a crispinette (a kind of decorative net) suspended from a hat that was almost pill-box in shape and held in place by a "barbette" strap under the chin.

The lower classes tended to wear less colourful, less elaborate versions of the clothes their masters wore. They could not afford expensive fabrics like silk, and their woollen garments were made of poorer quality coarse cloth. Men wore a shorter "smock" tunic and possibly a leather surcoat, with the animal hair still attached on the outside. Their leather boots were shorter, and worn over their stockings and breeches.

Peasant women wore long woollen dresses and short ankle boots, covering their shoulders with a rough shawl when it was cold. Generally, what distinguished a peasant from a nobleman at a glance was the colour of their clothing.

Peasant garb was drab, while the nobility wore green, gold and scarlet.

As more merchants and tradesmen began to acquire greater wealth, they aspired to dress like nobles and "sumptuary" laws were introduced, reserving certain styles, fabrics and colours for the upper classes. Later in the Middle Ages, there were even "fashion wardens" on the streets checking that unlikely looking characters had the right to wear the clothes they had on!

RICHARD DE MONTFICHET, BARON OF STANSTED

Like many of the other barons, Montfichet was a relatively young man (probably only in his early twenties) at the time of Magna Carta. Despite his youth, he formed part of the powerful group from the south-east of England. Montfichet's estates included custody of the royal forests in Essex, although these were reclaimed by the Crown from time to time as punishment for perceived misdemeanours by the Montfichet family.

The son of Richard de Montfichet – who served King Richard I – Montfichet was born some time in the 1190s. He was old enough to take the field of battle for King John in Poitou during his disastrous campaign in France of 1214, although he was firmly on the side of the rebel barons in June 1215.

Montfichet was captured at Lincoln in 1217 but recovered his lands and rights – including the Essex forests and the manor of Wraysbury in Buckinghamshire (situated on the River Thames very close to Runnymede) – when he swore allegiance to King Henry III after Prince Louis had returned to

France. He served in a number of official capacities, including as Sheriff of Essex and Hertfordshire, and bore witness to two of Henry's reissues of Magna Carta. He died in 1267, aged well over 70. Along with Roger Bigod, he was one of the longest-living of the 25 Magna Carta barons.

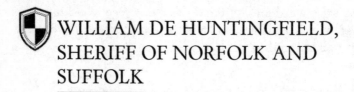

WILLIAM DE HUNTINGFIELD, SHERIFF OF NORFOLK AND SUFFOLK

A man who should have been one of King John's most loyal supporters, William de Huntingfield was a sheriff and a justice, travelling from town to town to set up court, resolve disputes and sit in judgement on the king's behalf.

This, it could be said, is something that any nobleman of his seniority might be expected to do, but in 1203, King John put Huntingfield in charge of Dover Castle. As castellan at Dover, he was responsible for defending one of the most strategically important strongholds in the country – the castle served not only as a garrison for the policing of a particular locality, but was also the first line of defence against invasion from the Continent. The fact that King John held Huntingfield's son and daughter hostage to ensure that their father did a good job would not have been apparent to everyone.

Yet, Huntingfield was still one of the nobles who accompanied the king on his ill-fated French military adventure in 1214. By that time, like so many of his peers, Huntingfield may have been heavily in debt to the Crown, having promised various payments in order either to acquire vacant lands and titles, or perhaps simply in order to retain those that were already his.

The following year, when Huntingfield was probably

around 40 years old, he committed himself to the barons' cause. His age would have made him one of the more senior members of the rebel alliance. He was captured at Lincoln in 1217, though his vassals raised the required ransom and he was released. Huntingfield is believed to have died some time around 1225.

THE BISHOPS

For King John, or any monarch, to govern England effectively – or to have any hope of surviving on the throne for any length of time – it was essential to have the Church on his side. The majority of people were deeply religious, either because they were pressured into respecting the Church through fear of becoming social outcasts, because they relied on the Church as they worked on estates owned by the clergy or because they had real faith and a genuine love (or fear) of God. The Church and the clergy were thus vitally important in keeping control of the population, and religion was an integral part of medieval politics.

Ultimate control of the clergy should, of course, have been out of the king's hands. King John was subordinate to the pope in religious matters, so to exert control over the clergy, the king either had to have the blessing of the pope in the major decisions he took in running the country, or to have the clergy on his side. Because it was recognized that the clergy played such a vital role in running the country, the king had to have a say in who took on the top jobs in the Church. While the clergy were ostensibly free to elect their own bishops and archbishops (Clause 1 of Magna Carta guaranteed this), it wasn't too difficult for the king to force the clergy to elect the man he wanted. The pope, too, could be induced to endorse such an official with promises of land, money or, perhaps, support for a crusade.

King John's father, Henry II, thought it would be a good idea to place his illegitimate son Geoffrey in the post of Bishop of Lincoln. However, Geoffrey was not ordained, meaning that he was unable to officiate at religious ceremonies. When Geoffrey's half-brother became King Richard I, the king insisted that Geoffrey take Holy Orders and become a proper priest. He was subsequently appointed Archbishop of York.

The clergy were important to the running of the country in other ways, too. The great cathedrals, abbeys and monasteries were also seats of learning. The major universities grew around these religious establishments and the clergy were the best-educated men in the country. They were able to advise not only on matters of religion, but also on legal and procedural matters. The lawyers and administrators who formed the king's "civil service" were either clergymen or had studied under and been trained by clergymen.

Clergymen were present, therefore, at every level of society throughout the realm, from the most humble parish priest to the most exalted archbishop. The Church was a visible institution that ordinary people certainly couldn't ignore. At the beginning of the thirteenth century, aside from the parish churches, there were more than a dozen abbeys and monasteries scattered around London. These live on in the names of districts such as Blackfriars, Greyfriars and Whitefriars.

Yet, the Church and the monarch seldom worked together in complete harmony. King Henry II had appointed an old friend Thomas Becket as Archbishop of Canterbury when the previous incumbent died in 1162. Becket had served the previous archbishop, Theobold of Bec, in a number of different roles, including Archdeacon of Canterbury, and had proved to be such a competent administrator that he was recommended to become Henry's Lord Chancellor in 1155. Henry doubtless believed that having Becket in place would give him greater control over the Church, not least because Becket had been away from the Church for seven years and he was liable to be out of touch with Church politics. Henry could not have been more wrong – his old friend stood loyal to the Church. The two men came into conflict over the way Henry raised taxes and whether clergymen accused of crimes should be liable to the king's justice or should be tried in Church courts.

The disputes raged out of control, with both men appealing to the pope who supported Becket, but needed Henry's assistance in his conflict with Frederick I, Holy Roman Emperor. He encouraged the two to negotiate a solution. Meanwhile, Becket fled to France in 1164 under the protection of Henry's enemy King Louis VII – from here he excommunicated anyone who took the king's side in the confrontation. By 1170, matters had calmed a little and Becket returned to England, but the dispute rumbled on until Henry complained to his court using words that have been reported, probably erroneously, as "Will no one rid me of this troublesome priest?" Whatever his actual words were, they were taken as a command by four of his knights, who rode to Canterbury and murdered Becket in the cathedral.

King John had his own problems with the clergy, especially when his preferred choice for the role of Archbishop of Canterbury was overruled by the pope in 1205. The pope consecrated his own choice, Stephen Langton, in June 1207, whereupon King John declared anyone in England who recognized Langton as archbishop to be a public enemy. In the spring of 1208, with the situation becoming ever more fraught, the pope placed all of England under an interdict and excommunicated King John.

The excommunication didn't seem to trouble John too much, but the interdict – whereby the clergy were banned from conducting normal religious duties – was a real thorn in his side. John's barons were increasingly perturbed by the situation as it caused unrest amongst the people on their estates who had to continue paying their tithes to the Church without receiving the benefit of proper rites from the priesthood. On the plus side for John, with the Crown having confiscated the estates belonging to the Church, he was enjoying a rich source of revenue. Eventually, in 1213, John gave in and Langton became Archbishop of Canterbury. John paid reparations to the pope and his excommunication was lifted, although he had to swear to defend the Church, and basically became a vassal of the pope.

John's problems with Langton, however, were not yet over. In Westminster in 1213, Langton met with some of the barons and read them the text of King Henry I's Coronation Charter, issued 113 years before. It proclaimed that the monarch would abide by certain laws, particularly concerning the rights and liberties of the nobility. It was Langton who promoted the notion that the barons should present the king with a list of demands, paving the way for Magna Carta.

It is no surprise, therefore, that Langton, as Archbishop of Canterbury, was heavily involved in peace negotiations between the rebel barons and King John or that he stood witness to the charter. In fact, there were more clergymen involved in ratifying Magna Carta than there were barons. Including Langton, there were 12 bishops or archbishops and 20 abbots, compared to just 25 barons and it is no accident that the very first clause of the charter grants that "the English church shall be free".

 WILLIAM MARSHAL

Born in 1190, William Marshal was the son of William, Earl of Pembroke, Marshal of England. William the elder was one of the most influential and celebrated warrior knights who ever lived. He had served Henry II, Henry the Younger and Richard I. Given that William's loyalty to Richard made him an unlikely ally of King John, John held his son as hostage to guarantee his loyalty.

William Marshal (the son) was, therefore, a reluctant guest of King John from 1205 until 1212, when John's need for his father's military support secured young William's freedom. When the confrontation with the barons developed in 1215, King John had the backing of William, Earl of Pembroke, but his son stood against the king.

When King John rejected Magna Carta, young William fought on the side of the barons but, when Prince Louis refused to guarantee him his family estates at the outcome of the hostilities, he changed sides. After the death of King John, when his father had been appointed Regent over the young King Henry III, the two Williams fought side by side at the battle of Lincoln.

When his father died in 1219, William inherited the title of Marshal of England and Earl of Pembroke, as well as estates in Ireland. He married in 1214, but his first wife died only two years later while pregnant with his son. Suspicions persist that she was murdered by an enemy in a land dispute. William married again in 1224, to none other than Princess Eleanor, sister of Henry III. He was 34 and she was only nine. They had no children, William dying seven years later. He was buried alongside his father in the Temple Church, London.

ISABELLA OF ANGOULÊME, QUEEN OF ENGLAND

Married to King John when he was 34 and she was only 12, Isabella was the only child of Audemar, Count of Angoulême. Marriage seemed like a good idea to John since the lands that his new bride would bring to their marriage were strategically important in maintaining the link between the southern part of his Aquitaine duchy and his Normandy estates in the north. They would also help to consolidate his eastern borders.

Renowned for her beauty, with blonde hair and blue eyes, Isabella was a dutiful wife to King John, providing him with that which his first wife could not – a son and heir. In fact, Isabella gave birth to two sons: Henry, who would become King Henry III, and Richard, Earl of Cornwall. There were also three daughters: Joan, who would become Queen of Scotland; Isabella, a future wife of Emperor Frederick II of Hohenstaufen; and Eleanor, Countess of Pembroke and Leicester.

Isabella was also of great use to John, working with his mother as a diplomat in his dealings with his noblemen in their home territories. John and Isabella's daughter, Joan, was betrothed to Hugh X of Lusignan – the son of the man Isabella had been about to marry before John swept her off to England.

When John died in 1216, Isabella ensured that Henry was crowned. She then left the nine-year-old king in the care of William Marshal, setting off across the Channel to escort Joan to her wedding. Instead of marrying Joan to Hugh, however, Isabella married Hugh herself. Isabella and Hugh's subsequent claims to territory in the Poitevin region later brought her into conflict with her own son, Henry, who launched a disastrous military campaign against the couple in 1230.

Isabella had nine more children with Hugh and, like John's mother, was extremely active in the politics and administration of her lands. She retired to Fontevrault Abbey – again like Eleanor – where she died in 1246.

GEOFFREY DE SAYE, LORD OF WEST GREENWICH

Family ties were certainly one of the things that united the rebel barons, along with a hatred for King John, a desire for justice, the chance to secure their own lands and the opportunity for financial gain. Family feuds, on the other hand, had to be set aside.

Geoffrey de Saye had to swallow a little of his pride, as did his cousin Geoffrey de Mandeville, when they fought on the same side against the king – their families had fought for years over control of estates in Essex. Saye's father had been granted the lands when he had appealed to King Richard I to resolve the territorial dispute in 1189. The king demanded a huge price of 7,000 marks for this service and Saye was unable to pay. Consequently, the estate was awarded elsewhere, eventually falling into the hands of Geoffrey de Mandeville.

In 1214, when his father died, Geoffrey de Saye appealed to King John – with whom he had fought in France – offering 15,000 marks for the estate to be given over to him. Although the king made moves to find out if this could be arranged, doubtless tempted by the price on offer, events probably overtook him.

Thus the two Geoffreys found themselves allied with the rebels. After the death of King John and Prince Louis's return to France, Saye swore fealty to King Henry III in 1217, before setting off on crusade to the Holy Land two years later. He also made a pilgrimage to Santiago de Compostela in 1223. Saye died in 1230, in his seventies, while campaigning with King Henry in France.

 # DURHAM

Durham Cathedral is regarded as an outstanding example of Norman architecture, the cathedral having been founded in 1098, on the site of a previous Saxon church. Durham Castle, once the palace of the Bishop of Durham and now part of Durham University, stands directly opposite the cathedral.

As part of the Durham Cathedral Muniments collection, Durham University Library holds three copies of Magna Carta. One was issued by Henry III (or rather by a regent acting on his behalf) in 1216 and is the only surviving copy of the 1216 charter. The second Durham copy was issued in 1225, again by Henry III but this time when the king had come of age. The final Durham charter is from 1300, issued during the reign of King Edward I.

 # OXFORD

There are no less than six copies of Magna Carta in Oxford, including five in the Bodleian Library. Of these, three are from the 1217 issue: one bears the seal of Henry III's regent, William Marshal; one is sealed by the young king's guardian, papal legate Guala Bicchieri; and one carries the seals of both Marshal and Bicchieri. The fourth copy is from 1225 and the fifth from 1300. Another copy of the 1300 issue of the charter is held at Oriel College, Oxford.

 WILLIAM DE LANVALLEI, LORD OF WALKERN AND STANDWAY CASTLE

Like so many of the English nobility, Lanvallei's family had served the Crown for generations. The family estates in Hertfordshire, Bedfordshire and the south-east of England had been granted to William's ancestor who held posts in the administration of Henry II. In 1214, William was with King John, fighting in France, but by the following year he had been recruited into the ranks of the rebels. Family ties are probably at the heart of his decision to stand against the king. William's wife, Maud, was the niece of Robert FitzWalter (the leader of the Magna Carta barons), while his mother was aunt to another leading rebel, Geoffrey de Mandeville.

In the summer of 1216, with the war against King John raging and Prince Louis of France declared King of England (although not crowned) in St Paul's Cathedral in London, William was made custodian of Colchester Castle in Essex, a property to which he believed he had ancestral rights and for which he had been fighting for many years.

Unfortunately, he didn't have much time to enjoy his new home, as he died the same year, probably in his early thirties.

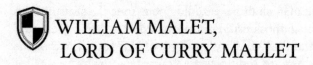

WILLIAM MALET, LORD OF CURRY MALLET

Although his mounting debts were a major cause for concern by the time of Magna Carta, Malet had previously been a stalwart supporter of the monarchy. He was another baron driven to rebel by his financial situation and the punitive taxes paid to the king.

As a young man Malet had accompanied King Richard I on crusade in 1190, participating in the siege of Acre (a port in the Holy Land north-east of Jerusalem) in 1191. His appointment as Sheriff of Somerset and Dorset was made by King John in 1209, and he served in that capacity for three years.

By 1214, Malet was heavily in debt, mainly to King John, and he agreed to fight with the king in France. He supplied a squadron of 10 knights, along with 20 other soldiers, in return for the wiping out of his debts to the Crown. It may be that John reneged on this deal, or came up with more taxes to burden the beleaguered Malet, because the baron joined the rebels in 1215.

Aside from being nominated as one of the 25 Magna Carta guarantors, Malet played no great role in the war itself. He died in December 1215, aged around 40.

FREE MEN

The term "free man" crops up many times in the Magna Carta, not least in Clause 39 where it is stated that:

No free man shall be seized or imprisoned, or stripped of his rights or possessions, or outlawed or exiled, or deprived of his standing in any way, nor will we proceed with force against him, or send others to do so, except by the lawful judgment of his equals or by the law of the land.

Although it may seem as though this clause is granting everyone what we would today consider to be basic human rights, not everyone actually counted as a "free man". A free man was not an ordinary peasant, a term that encompassed most of the population of England in 1215. Rather, "free man" referred to someone who lived on the fringe of the feudal system but who was not bound in servitude to the lord of the manor. A free man's freedom came from the fact that he owned his own tract of land, was the freeholder, and worked that patch of land, however small, to support his family.

A free man was not free from all obligations to the community. He would, for example, still have to pay the tithe to his local clergyman and other taxes that might be levied upon him, but he was not "owned" lock, stock and barrel by the local nobleman.

The term lives on in the modern world in the form of a number of English surnames. "Freeman" is the most obvious, but "Franklin" means much the same thing, derived from the Middle English "frankeleyn", or a form thereof, which combines the Old French "franc" (meaning free) and a version of the German suffix "lein". Given the way that the language melting pot worked in the Middle Ages, it's not difficult to see how Franklin evolved as a surname for a free man. "Fry" or "Frey" are other names associated with the status of a free man, derived from the Germanic word "frei", meaning "free", and the Old English word "frig", meaning "free born".

The lowest of the free men lived lives little different from those of the general peasantry, but some owned enough land to allow them to stand on a slightly higher rung of the social ladder without them actually attaining the rank or status of nobleman.

Another form of free man was a "free tenant", who held a form of lease contract from his local landlord under which he farmed the land in return for an annual rent. While a free tenant did not have as much actual freedom as a freeholder, he was, at least, able to raise whatever livestock he chose, could leave the area if he wanted to travel further afield to buy or sell goods and did not need permission to marry a wife of his own choosing.

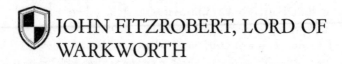 JOHN FITZROBERT, LORD OF WARKWORTH

FitzRobert was one of the most powerful of the northern barons. He owned estates in Northumberland, along the Scottish border, as well as Clavering Castle and its associated estates in Essex. The FitzRobert family had served the Plantagenet kings loyally for generations, Henry II having granted FitzRobert's grandfather a castle at Warkworth in Northumberland in 1158.

As was the case with many of the barons, FitzRobert's loyalty to the Crown left him in a real quandary. King John had granted a number of estates to FitzRobert and he had served the king as Sheriff of Norfolk and Suffolk, a position he held when the barons began their action against the king.

FitzRobert was not, therefore, in the vanguard of the revolt, but his wealth and status afforded him a great deal of respect from his friends in the north and he was nominated as one of "the 25". After the king reneged on Magna Carta, FitzRobert was left with no choice but to fight against the

Crown. However, his belief in the institute of the monarchy was such that, when the rebels were defeated at Lincoln after the death of King John, he was one of the first to pay homage to John's son, King Henry III.

The great wealth and wide-ranging influence that FitzRobert's family had acquired over the years doubtless made his submission most welcome and his actions surely persuaded others to follow suit. FitzRobert went on to serve the new king as Sheriff of Northumberland. He died at the age of about 50 in 1240.

PRINCESS ISABELLA OF SCOTLAND

Along with her sister, Margaret, Isabella had a direct connection with Magna Carta through Clause 59 – both girls were held hostage by King John from 1209 to ensure that their father did not take up arms against him. They were imprisoned in Corfe Castle in Dorset, where their incarceration was actually more of a house arrest. Given that teenage girls of their age – Isabella was 14 and her sister 16 – were commonly sent away from home, being held hostage was probably no more of an ordeal for them than becoming wards or ladies-in-waiting would have been.

In Corfe, at least, the sisters were kept together and, after a couple of years, they were joined by Eleanor of Brittany, who was being held by John to ensure that she could not pursue her legitimate claim to territory across the Channel or even to his throne in England.

As part of John's agreement with the girls' father when he took responsibility for Margaret and Isabella, the king had promised to find suitable husbands for them. In Isabella's case, this simply never happened and when she was released after John's death, she returned to Scotland. In 1225, she did eventually marry Roger Bigod, heir to the Earl of Norfolk. By the time of her marriage, she was 30 years old and her husband was just 13.

The couple lived in Scotland until Roger was old enough to inherit his estates. Despite the fact that he tried to have their marriage annulled in order to take another wife – Isabella having failed to provide him with an heir – their later years together seem to have been reasonably happy ones. Following her death sometime around the mid-1250s, Isabella was buried near her sister in Blackfriars in London and, when he died in 1270, Roger was buried in Thetford. Isabella and Roger's hearts are said to have been buried together at the Church of St Michael the Archangel in Framlingham.

 SAER DE QUINCY, EARL OF WINCHESTER

Born around 1170 to Sir Robert de Quincy – who was in the service of William the Lion, King of Scotland – Saer de Quincy spent his formative years north of the border, where he, too, served the Scottish kings at court.

When his father inherited lands in England, Quincy went south and fought for King Richard I in France in 1198, as well as for King John in Normandy in 1203, where he was in joint command of the fortress at Vaudreuil. When he and his fellow castellan, his cousin Robert FitzWalter, surrendered the castle without a fight, but apparently on the orders of King John, they were held to ransom by the French. King John, of course, refused to contribute to the ransom demand.

In 1207, Quincy inherited the title Earl of Winchester, along with its associated estates, through his wife, Margaret. By 1211, he was back in Scotland as an emissary of King John, but also leading a military force to put down insurrections as part of a campaign mounted by William the Lion.

Quincy clearly held grudges against King John, however, not least because – over and above the matter of the ransom – the king had denied him property that should have come his way as part of his wife's inheritance.

When the rebel barons rose against John in 1215, Quincy was quick to join them and was one of their number who travelled to France to persuade Prince Louis that he would have their backing should he make an attempt on the English throne.

Quincy was captured when the barons were defeated at the Battle of Lincoln, but later released under the general amnesty. He served King Henry II before embarking on the Fifth Crusade in 1219. He became ill in Egypt and died there towards the end of the year.

 # FOOD

In high society, eating was part of the ritual and routine of castle life for the family and staff of a nobleman. Mealtimes were a chance for the lord to be seen by his staff and servants, letting them know who was boss, and it was an opportunity for him to entertain guests who were either visiting or passing through on their travels.

Meals were taken in the Great Hall of the castle, which would be laid out with a long table for the lord, his family, their guests and their castle chaplain or visiting clergy. Others would sit at trestle tables that could be folded away for storage when not needed. The table to the right of the lord's table was the most prestigious place to be seated, and the further away from the "top" table you were, the lower you ranked in the social pecking order.

The lord's table sat on a dais, so that he and his family were physically "above" those who were deemed to be beneath them socially. The table would be laid with a cloth, draped lower at the side where the diners sat so that they could wipe their hands on it, and there were individual seats. At the other tables, diners sat at benches that later on might also serve as beds for the many staff who slept in the Great Hall at night.

The top table was set with a salt dish (one of the rules of etiquette was that you should not dip your food in the salt, making it go lumpy with food debris), goblets for wine or ale, and spoons. Forks were not used at the beginning of the thirteenth century and diners were expected to bring their own knives. Anything that could not be cut with a knife and picked up with the fingers, such as soup, was eaten with a spoon.

Food was served on platters – silver for the lord and his most esteemed guests, wooden for everyone else – but eaten off "trenchers" of flat bread that served as plates. Actual plates were not generally used in England until the fourteenth century. For soup or stew, a round loaf would be scooped out to form a trencher "bowl". It was not the done thing actually to eat your trencher, as these were collected after the meal and later either distributed to the poor or fed to the pigs.

As fingers were used for eating, servants circulated with bowls and pitchers of water so that everyone could wash their hands. This might also happen between courses.

There were rituals involved in carving meat, which was an art that the squires were expected to master. The lord and his guests were served in a set order, with high-ranking visiting clergymen served first.

Breakfast was a light meal served early in the morning after mass and would usually consist of white bread, sliced cold meat, cheese and wine. Staff and retainers would have cheaper bread, ale or cider, the quality of food generally deteriorating the further you sat from the top table.

Dinner was the main meal of the day, probably served by noon at the latest. It would consist of two or three courses, with two or three different types of meat. A special dinner feast would involve many more courses and the meat on offer could range from venison or wild boar shot on hunting trips, to beef, mutton or pork. Game that was shot was, of course, shot with a bow and arrow. There were no firearms in England until around 150 years after Magna Carta.

There were also fish and fowl served in the early thirteenth century that probably wouldn't go down too well at the average dinner table nowadays. These could include starling, heron, stork, cormorant, swan, peacock or the more familiar to us duck or chicken. Fish served at table (especially on Wednesdays, Fridays, Saturdays or during Lent, when the church decreed that no meat should be eaten) included salmon, trout, haddock, cod, eels, sardines, dogfish, dolphin and whale.

For dessert there would be cheese, wafers, jellies, cookies and spiced wine. This was the only drink normally served hot and the spices were used to cover the fact that the wine might have turned sour. Food was spiced with pepper, mustard, garlic or cloves, again mainly to disguise the taste of meat that might have started to turn bad. There were no refrigerators in those days and keeping food fresh was a real problem. Meat was stored in salt in the hope that it would last through the winter months. Much of the livestock was slaughtered in late autumn, fodder for the animals during the winter being scarce.

Most meat, especially birds, were cooked and served as a

whole animal, whenever possible, with the head still on, or with the head sewn back on after cooking so that it could be presented in the Great Hall with some ceremony (and everyone able to recognize what they were about to eat).

Supper was served at sundown and was usually just one course with a few side dishes and spiced wine.

The range and quantity of food varied down through the social ranks, with most aspiring to eat like the nobility but few able to afford such luxury. Peasant food could be extremely basic. While the rich ate meat, pies and pastries, the poor relied on vegetables. A stock pot was kept constantly simmering over the fire, to which a few vegetables, roots or even leaves such as nettles could be added to freshen it up before eating.

The most common vegetables – and vegetables were looked upon as commoners' food – were cabbage, peas, beans and onions. The Romans had introduced asparagus centuries before, but this was not widely grown, while some other vegetables, like leeks and cucumbers, were thought to be bad for you. Doubtless, when times were hard, they were a welcome addition to the stock pot nonetheless. There were no potatoes, which would not arrive from South America via Spain until the sixteenth century, and no tomatoes for the same reason.

The bread eaten by peasants was far different from that consumed at the lord's table. It was baked using rye or barley rather than the fine wheat flour used for the nobles' loaf, and at times the rough flour used in peasant bread would be supplemented with peas or beans.

As well as vegetable broth or stew from the pot, peasants ate porridge, oat cakes and cheese curds, washed down with ale, cider or mead. If they were lucky, they might be allowed to take fish from a local river, but they were only permitted to take those types that did not normally make their way to the lord's table – trout and salmon were not for the lower classes.

The poorest peasants did not keep their own livestock – animals ate food that they might just as well eat themselves – but, as well as looking after their overlord's animals, a lucky few might have some chickens or even keep rabbits. At the time of year when the pigs were slaughtered, a peasant family might have a few cuts of pork or some bacon.

 # HEREFORD

The Cathedral Church of St Mary the Virgin and St Ethelbert the King, more commonly known as Hereford Cathedral, stands on a site that has been a place of Christian worship for more than a thousand years. Churches here have been built, destroyed and rebuilt over the centuries as various warring factions vented their aggression on the fabric of the building.

The oldest part of the current building dates back to around 1079, although there have been many alterations and additions since then, turning it into one of the most important cathedrals in the west of England. As well as admiring its magnificent architecture, visitors to the cathedral may also have the opportunity to study two famous documents that are housed there. One is Mappa Mundi, a fascinating map of the world, or as much of the world as was known when it was created in 1285. It is the largest medieval artefact of its kind anywhere. The other document is one of the best preserved of the oldest eight copies of Magna Carta.

The Hereford charter is from the 1217 issue, which has its own claim to fame. This charter came about when the war with the barons had ended and Prince Louis had returned to France, having agreed to a peace treaty known as the Treaty of Lambeth. There were still problems between the Crown and the barons and the 1217 charter formed part of the peace treaty. It is different from both the 1215 original and the amended 1216 version, demonstrating how the charter would evolve throughout its various incarnations. Clauses that were deemed to be impractical or otherwise unacceptable were altered or removed. Some of the ongoing disputes concerned the management of the royal forests, their boundaries and the way in which they were subject to a separate legal system.

To address some of these areas, a separate "Charter of the Forests" was created. The 1217 charter carried for the first time the title *Magna Carta Libertatum* – "The Great Charter of Liberties", to be known forever more as Magna Carta.

ROGER AND HUGH BIGOD, EARLS OF NORFOLK

Roger Bigod and his son, Hugh – who would go on to inherit his father's title – had a long, and not entirely happy, association with the kings of England. In an inheritance maze as complex as you could imagine, Roger had inherited his earldom from his father, Hugh, who had been granted the title in the days of King Stephen, probably around 1141.

Roger's father, Hugh, abandoned his wife and married again, producing two more sons – Hugh and William. By the time that Hugh (Roger's father) died in 1177, King Henry II was on the throne and, because Hugh had intended that his sons by his second marriage should inherit, Roger had a fight on his hands. Henry took advantage of this to exact revenge for old Hugh having taken part in a rebellion against him in 1173, and confiscated the lands until the dispute between Roger, Hugh and William could be resolved. Given that Henry was then able to enjoy revenue from the properties, resolution of the dispute was always going to come later rather than sooner. Roger did not come into his rightful inheritance until Richard I became king in 1189, and only then when he paid handsomely for the privilege.

Nevertheless, Roger served Richard well and later showed loyalty to King John, fighting on his behalf in Normandy amongst other places. By the time of Magna Carta, however, Roger and his son, Hugh, saw their place as being with the rebel barons. Roger was about 70 years old and owed significant amounts to the king in scutage and other fees and taxes, something that made the decision to stand against King John all the easier.

During the ensuing war, King John captured the Bigods' family seat of Framlingham Castle and they were not able to return to their estates until 1217. Roger Bigod died in 1221 and his son, Hugh, enjoyed the title of Earl of Norfolk only until 1225 when he, too, died. The earldom passed on to his son, Roger.

PRINCESS MARGARET OF SCOTLAND

Clause 59 of Magna Carta makes reference to Margaret and Isabella, sisters of Alexander II of Scotland. Born around 1193, Margaret was just 16 when her father, William the Lion, King of Scotland, fell foul of England's King John. The dispute between them was eventually settled in John's favour when William was forced to sue for peace, handing over a huge cash settlement. He also handed over his daughters to become wards – effectively hostages – of the English king.

The girls were not flung into rat-infested dungeons, but were kept in secure comfort, John having promised William to arrange suitable marriages for them. Margaret was to be married to John's own son, Henry, but this never happened. He clearly had the political upper hand and military superiority when it came to dealing with the Scottish king, so decided to wait until the opportunity arose for him to marry the Scottish princesses to husbands through which the unions would bring him some advantage.

When William the Lion roared his last, in December 1214, the barons brought the Scots on side by forcing the issue of the marriages, although John, of course, reneged on the whole Magna Carta agreement anyway.

After John's death, Margaret eventually married, at the age of around 28, to Hubert de Burgh, the Justiciar of the Kingdom of England. She became Margaret of Scotland, Countess of Kent. The couple had one child, also called Margaret and known as "Megotta", who died when she was a teenager.

Margaret once again found herself deprived of her liberty, this time when her husband fell from grace though he was ultimately restored to the nobility. She outlived her husband, inheriting his lands when he died. Margaret died in 1259 and was buried alongside her husband in Blackfriars in London.

 ROBERT DE VERE, EARL OF OXFORD

Although not among the most powerful of the barons, Vere should have been a man that King John could count on for loyalty and support. Even after his marriage to Isabel de Bolebec, when Vere gained control of the estates that his wife had inherited, he was still not one of the major land-owning barons. However, his family had served the Crown loyally for generations.

Vere inherited his titles from his brother and it was in coming into his inheritance that his loyalty to King John was first tested. The king demanded a hefty fee, or "relief" tax, from Vere following the death of his brother in 1214, but would not confirm Vere's appointment to the titles until after Runnymede, by which time Vere was firmly in the rebel camp.

When the barons went to war with the king following his rejection of Magna Carta, things did not go well for Vere. In the spring of 1216, King John's forces laid siege to Vere's family seat at Castle Hedingham, taking the fortress after three days. Vere was not present, but was promised he would not be harmed if he went to the king and reaffirmed his oaths of allegiance. This Vere did, although he kept his vows not a second longer than he needed to, supporting Prince Louis against King John and fighting on with the rebels even after John's death. He eventually swore fealty to the Crown again after the general amnesty in 1217.

Vere died around the middle of October 1221, probably aged in his late fifties.

 # HOUSING

At the time of Magna Carta, most people in England lived in small villages consisting of a few rough houses gathered near a manor house or a church, with a castle never too far away in the distance.

The houses were very basic, built using materials that could be found in the vicinity – although taking wood from any forest belonging to the feudal overlord might require permission for which a fee in the form of money, goods or labour would inevitably be charged.

Houses had an earth floor, part of which might even have been dug out below ground level to provide something of a starting point for the walls and potentially give two levels to the dwelling. The walls were built using timber to create a strong frame that was then filled using wattle and daub. This consisted of thin branches woven into a lattice – the wattle – and attached to the frame. The walls would then resemble screens or fences, and would not be much good at keeping out wind and rain, so they were then coated on the outside, or "daubed" with mud. Heavy clay was good, because it would stick to the lattice, but this was not always readily available and, in warm weather, it would dry out, crack and crumble. To make the daub more flexible, and to help waterproof it, the mud or clay was mixed with horse or cow dung. Water would be added to make it easy to work (yes, by hand) and the gooey, smelly mixture was then plastered onto the wattle. When it dried, it made a sound plaster that kept the elements at bay.

Windows in a peasant cottage were simply square holes left in the wall that could be covered with a wattle frame or wooden shutter. The doorway would have either a wooden door or an animal hide covering the opening.

The roof would be made of thatch or turf with a hole cut in it to let out the smoke from the cooking fire, which would also heat the house.

Having two levels to the earth floor – even if one was only slightly higher than the other – meant that the family could use the upper level to bed down at night, sleeping on straw or bracken, while any livestock that they had was brought in for the night and occupied the lower level. A peasant house was not likely to have even the most rudimentary of furniture.

At the other end of the social scale, the local baron lived in a castle built of stone. Prior to the Norman invasion in 1066, there were very few stone castles in England, most being wooden fortresses in the "motte and bailey" style.

This type of castle involved taking advantage of a natural feature, such as a small hill, and creating a much larger mound, or "motte". On this was built a wooden keep on several floors, to where the nobleman and his family could retreat if their home came under attack. There were several other wooden buildings, with either thatch or shingle roofs in a courtyard – the "bailey" – that were surrounded by a palisade and a ditch.

While these castles afforded the occupants some protection, they were vulnerable to fire, flaming arrows being used to set the thatched roofs and wooden walls alight as a besieging force camped safely beyond the ditch. In order to keep the restless natives subdued, the Normans built these castles first in wood, for speed, and then in stone, for security, expanding and extending the castles as they did so.

The main part of a stone castle was the first-floor Great Hall. This was where the occupants of the castle gathered for meals, for entertainment and, in the case of staff and servants, to sleep. There was a large fireplace in the Great Hall, which, by the thirteenth century had a proper chimney so that the hall did not fill with smoke. Stone walls were decorated with tapestries and flags as a mark of the lord's status, and the floor would be strewn with reeds or rushes to soak up water and mud from wet boots. The rushes could be swept out and replaced to freshen up the hall.

The kitchens were generally in the basement, or possibly in another castle building altogether, while upstairs were the apartments for the lord's family, guests and perhaps his highest-ranking officials. Some of these rooms would have fireplaces and some would have windows with shutters that could be pulled at night. These would eventually be supplemented by glass in the windows.

Even in the lord's chambers, decor was spartan by modern standards. The walls and floor were most likely to be bare stone, although the floor might be made of wooden planks. Wall hangings, as in the Great Hall, would brighten the rooms and the floor might be softened with a rug or two. There would be very little furniture – a bed, possibly a small table and chair and perhaps a night stand with a bowl and a pitcher of water for washing. There was no bathroom or running water. Chamber pots were used, or there might be a small chamber nearby where anyone needing to go to the toilet used a hole in the wall that sent everything out into the moat surrounding the castle. Unless the moat was flushed through with running water from a stream, it wasn't the sort of place you would want to take a swim!

Not every lord lived in a castle, and some who owned castles preferred to live in a manor house close to the castle. Stone castles were cold and draughty places built for war. A manor house could provide more comfortable living.

Manor houses were either wooden-framed buildings that used much the same timber-frame building technique as was utilized for a peasant dwelling (though on a much grander scale), or were fortified houses made of stone.

Using brickwork rendered with plaster rather that wattle-and-daub was more expensive, but far stronger. Grand houses were two storeys high – the lord and his family would have the upper floor as their sleeping area while the servants bedded down in the Great Hall below (as they would in a castle).

A manor house might have a thatched roof, but a fortified manor would have a roof of slate or clay tiles like a castle building.

Even a stone manor house, however, could not be defended as effectively as a castle. It could be used, though, as a hunting lodge or to get away from castle life for a while –providing that the castle was close enough to run to if your enemies came riding over the hill!

LINCOLN

At the time of Magna Carta, Lincoln was one of the most important places in the realm. It had grown to become England's third-largest city, with a great castle boasting two mottes – one of only two such castles in the country, Lewes in Sussex being home to the other. The castle had been built by William the Conqueror on the site of an old Roman fortress. It was strategically important because Lincoln lay at a crossroads of old Roman roads and waterways, making it an important centre of communications. Holding Lincoln Castle was key to controlling routes north and south as well as to the east as far as the North Sea.

Lincoln also had one of the most impressive cathedrals in England. Although badly damaged by an earthquake in 1185, the cathedral was in the process of being rebuilt and enlarged when Magna Carta came along, the building programme stretching on until around 1235. The cathedral would become the highest building in the world, one of its spires making it taller than the Great Pyramid at Giza – although that spire was destroyed during a storm in 1549. Nevertheless, both before and after the loss of the spire, the cathedral was an impressively tall building. During the Second World War, when Lincolnshire was home to scores of Allied bomber bases, aircrews returning from missions over Germany used Lincoln Cathedral as a navigation aid. Even if there was low cloud, the tops of the towers could be seen poking up through the clouds.

Due to its position on major trade routes, Lincoln was a major centre for the wool and weaving industry, and a prosperous city. Lincoln cloth was renowned for its quality and became famous for its scarlet and green hues. King John's legendary nemesis, Robin Hood, famously wore "Lincoln green" as an outlaw in Sherwood Forest.

Lincoln's military strategic value, the formidable Lincoln Castle, the cathedral with its associated centre of education, as well as the wealth that was generated by and existed in the city inevitably brought war to its gates many times. King Stephen, when fighting off the challenge of King John's grandmother, Matilda, laid siege to Lincoln in 1141 and was captured during a bitter battle when Matilda's forces arrived to lift the siege.

It was in Lincoln that King William the Lion of Scotland paid homage to King John in 1200, and here, too, that Nicholaa de La Haye held the castle – as she did many times – against a besieging rebel army in 1216 (King John visiting her castle shortly before his death). Indeed, it was at Lincoln that the decisive battle of the First Barons' War was fought in 1217. Once again, Nicholaa was holding the castle while the forces of the rebel barons occupied the city surrounding the castle, putting it under siege. William the Marshal arrived at the head of an army, intent on surrounding the city and besieging the besiegers, but his men found a way in through the city walls and a bloody battle ensued. Many of the barons who had not already pledged their allegiance to the young King Henry III, with William the Marshal acting as regent for the nine-year-old king, were captured at Lincoln and returned to the royal fold.

While Lincoln had a vital part to play in the proceedings at the time of Magna Carta, its role did not end then and has continued to the present day. For centuries, an original copy of the 1215 issue of Magna Carta was held in Lincoln

Cathedral and nowadays is normally on display at Lincoln Castle. This is, perhaps, the most travelled copy of Magna Carta. In 1939 it was on display at the World Fair in New York, but the outbreak of the Second World War made it too risky a business to attempt to ship it back to the UK. Consequently, it spent most of the war safe in the vaults of the US Federal Reserve in Fort Knox, Kentucky. It was this copy that Winston Churchill proposed to give to America in a show of Anglo–US solidarity, and in the hope that it might tempt America – then neutral – to enter the war. Lincoln Cathedral, however, wanted its charter returned after the war and Churchill's plan never got off the ground.

The copy came back to England after the war but travelled once again to America in 2007 to be displayed in Virginia and Philadelphia. In 2009, it was shown at the Fraunces Tavern Museum in New York.

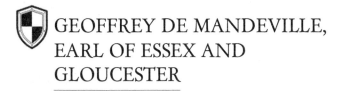

GEOFFREY DE MANDEVILLE, EARL OF ESSEX AND GLOUCESTER

Mandeville had more reason than most to despise King John and would surely have sided with the rebel barons even if the man deemed their leader, Robert FitzWalter, had not once intervened to save his life.

The story goes that, as a young man, Mandeville got into a fight and killed another, said to be a servant. King John insisted that he be tried for murder and Mandeville faced being hanged until Robert FitzWalter – to whose daughter Mandeville was married – turned up with 200 armed knights, leaving the king in no doubt as to what would happen if he made any attempt to hang FitzWalter's son-in-law.

Mandeville's wife, and FitzWalter's daughter, Matilda died in 1212 and King John suggested that it might be a good idea for Mandeville to remarry. As it happened, John had the perfect (in his eyes) candidate – his own first wife, Isabella, from whom he was now divorced. She was 18 years older than Mandeville, but she came with inherited lands and titles that would make him Earl of Gloucester. All he had to do was to pay the king 20,000 marks. It was an offer Mandeville couldn't refuse and he married Isabella in 1214, promising to pay the price in four instalments.

That, of course, was never going to happen. The following year, Mandeville followed his erstwhile father-in-law on the road to rebellion. In 1216, while still in his early twenties, Mandeville was killed fighting a French knight at a tournament in London.

WILLIAM HARDEL, SHERIFF AND MAYOR OF LONDON

Unlike the barons in the provinces, whose claims to land, wealth and titles relied on their ancestry and their family ties with each other, the Mayor of London was elected by his peers, and those had generally risen to prominence as merchants, traders and professionals.

William Hardel's family business was in wine. He had become a figure of some importance, not only in London's growing business community, but in its political circles as well, having served as Sheriff in 1207–8. Hardel held property in the Vintry area of the city (Vintry is still one of London's 25 wards – divisions for the purpose of political elections), which was the centre of the wine trade, and in Bishopsgate, also still one of London's wards.

Hardel, a man of influence with the wealthiest elite of London, had ties with Robert FitzWalter who was Lord of Baynard's Castle in the city. Preserving the city from the devastation of an urban war doubtless helped FitzWalter to persuade Hardel to join the rebel alliance.

It was Hardel, accompanied by FitzWalter, who led the people of London in paying homage to Prince Louis in St Paul's churchyard in June 1216.

ISABELLA OF GLOUCESTER, QUEEN OF ENGLAND

King John was first married, when he was 23 years old and still Prince John, to 16-year-old Isabella of Gloucester. The marriage was the brainwave of John's father, Henry II, who negotiated a deal with Isabella's father to help his youngest son lose the "Lackland" nickname that he had acquired.

William, Earl of Gloucester's only son, Robert, had died some years earlier, leaving Isabella and her three sisters liable each to inherit a third of their father's estates. King Henry offered the Gloucesters a step up the aristocratic ladder by marrying into royalty, but only if all of the land went to Isabella – and thence to John – when the old earl died.

Isabella and John were married in 1189 at Marlborough Castle, but this was to be a troubled union from the outset. The Gloucesters already had certain royal connections, the earl's father having been an illegitimate son of King Henry I. Isabella and John, therefore, shared a great grandfather, which was a close enough relationship for the Archbishop of Canterbury to declare the marriage unlawful. John appealed to the pope who allowed the marriage, but only under the strange proviso that the couple refrained from any sexual activity.

Whether John and Isabella adhered to the pope's instructions or not, they had no children together. John finally had the marriage annulled on the grounds of consanguinity and may have always intended to do so. He then sold the right to marry Isabella and the title of Earl of Gloucester to Geoffrey de Mandeville, Earl of Essex, for the enormous sum of 20,000 marks.

Isabella and Geoffrey stood against King John after he rejected Magna Carta. When Geoffrey died from wounds sustained during a tournament in 1216, Isabella was left in sole control of her own estates at last. She did marry again, to Hubert de Burgh, in 1217, but died a few months later and was buried at Canterbury.

HENRY DE BOHUN, EARL OF HEREFORD

Such was the infighting between the noble, not-so-noble and would-be-noble families of England around the beginning of the thirteenth century that the king was regularly called upon to resolve such disputes. Legal challenges over the possession of lands were often based on family members having had their lands confiscated by overlords or the Crown generations before. When family honour and, more importantly, money was concerned, however, the king's ruling only ever held until one of the parties died and an inheritance came up for grabs again.

If it sounds tedious, then it probably was, but King John would not have minded too much because, as in most other matters, he generally charged a fee for interceding. There was slightly more to it in the case of Henry de Bohun versus William Longespée, who was King John's half-brother. Longespée was granted lands and titles when Henry II recognised him as his son. A dedicated supporter of John, Longespée fought for him in Ireland, in Wales and in France, and remained loyal until the King's death. Longespée had launched a legal action claiming ownership of Bohun's lordship of Trowbridge in Wiltshire, on the basis that he was descended from an earlier incumbent.

This caused a major headache for Bohun, who had already fallen foul of King John when he was made Earl of Hereford in 1200. John had refused at that time to allow Bohun control of all the land and property traditionally associated with the title. During the Longespée legal action in 1212, Bohun attempted to delay proceedings and failed to appear at hearings, saying he was ill. As a result, the crown seized the disputed territory of Trowbridge and while John kept the property for himself, he allowed his half-brother to exact scutage fees from the tenants.

Bohun became another of the barons who, despite having a long family history of service to the Crown, so despised King John that he gave his support to the rebels. He was one of the barons captured at the Battle of Lincoln and afterwards swore allegiance to King Henry III.

Bohun died aged about 45, while on crusade to the Holy Land in 1220.

 SALISBURY

Of the four original copies of Magna Carta still in existence, the one that is displayed in the Chapter House of Salisbury Cathedral is the copy that has best stood the test of time over the past eight centuries. This is almost certainly the copy that was sent to the Sheriff of Wiltshire and it has been kept in Salisbury

Cathedral ever since it was created in 1215. However, that does not mean that it has always been kept in the same place.

Salisbury, known at the time of Magna Carta as "Sarum", has been in existence for around 5,000 years. The earliest settlement was on a hilltop not far from where the giant monoliths were erected at Stonehenge and Avebury, archaeologists having discovered evidence of a prehistoric settlement.

There is also evidence of an Iron Age hill fort dating back 2,400 years, and the Romans also used the site, as did the Saxons. However, the major fortifications on the hilltop were built by the Normans – a substantial motte-and-bailey castle, a stone wall enclosing the hilltop, and a cathedral.

The Norman castle at Salisbury was generally held by the king rather than being tenanted by one of his barons, and the castellan in charge of the castle on a day-to-day basis was the Sheriff of Wiltshire. The cathedral was built by Herman, Bishop of Salisbury and Saint Osmund – a cousin of William the Conqueror – who was Chancellor of England and responsible for the compilation of the Domesday book. He was canonized more than 300 years after his death and would become the patron saint of mental illness, paralysis, ruptures and toothache. Neither Herman nor Saint Osmund lived long enough to see the building work completed in 1092.

It was in this cathedral that Magna Carta was first archived, but it was not on this spot that it would stay. Old Sarum was to move off the hilltop and down onto the plain, becoming New Sarum and eventually known simply as Salisbury, with the building of a new Salisbury Cathedral beginning in 1221 – although the plans to move the cathedral down onto Salisbury Plain were approved by King Richard I in the early 1190s. The new cathedral took 38 years to build and holds numerous records. It has the tallest spire in Britain at 404 feet (123 metres), as well as the largest cloister, the biggest cathedral close and the oldest working clock in the world (dating from 1386).

The cathedral's greatest claim to fame, however, is its copy of the original 1215 Magna Carta. Archived for centuries, it was only rediscovered in 1812. This copy, while extremely well preserved, is also slightly different from the others. The handwriting is not in the same style, the other 1215 manuscripts having a formal appearance associated with charter documents – a kind of bureaucratic, government-issue style of the time. The style of the Salisbury charter differs in that it appears more like the kind of writing that would have been used in the manuscript pages of a book.

This has led people to believe that the Salisbury document may have been written by a monk or a member of the cathedral's clerical staff, the wording copied from another copy of the charter. The Salisbury version would then have had the king's seal attached at the royal court. While this may seem like a strange way of issuing the charter, it should be noted that King John's staff were under pressure to complete numerous copies, and creating one of these documents was a painstaking, exacting task.

At least 13 copies of the 1215 charter were issued, but it was probably expected that there would be one copy sent to each county, and perhaps some more besides. It could be that 40 copies would have been needed, although events moved too quickly for that to have happened. The Salisbury charter is, therefore, unique.

RICHARD AND GILBERT DE CLARE, EARLS OF HERTFORD AND EARLS OF GLOUCESTER

Richard de Clare was in his sixties by the time of Magna Carta and the barons' revolt but, despite his advancing years, was hugely influential due to the vast estates held by his family. He had held the title of Earl of Hertford, along with estates in Kent, Buckinghamshire, Norfolk and Northamptonshire, for more than 40 years and brought considerable military might to the barons' cause.

During the hostilities, he added yet more territory to his family's holdings when his wife, Amice, inherited the Gloucester estates and titles from her sister, Isabella (the former wife of King John) on Isabella's death in 1217. Amice was Richard's only wife and the couple spent a good deal of time apart, reportedly because the pope had ordered them to separate, their marriage having been judged unlawful due to consanguinity.

This certainly doesn't seem to have stopped them from producing a son and heir as Gilbert de Clare was born around 1180 and joined his father among the ranks of the barons. Gilbert was captured by William Marshal at the Battle of Lincoln in 1217. However, the two can hardly be described as bitter enemies since Gilbert married Marshal's daughter, Isabel a few months later when she had just turned 17 and Gilbert was in his late 30s.

Richard de Clare died in 1217 and Gilbert inherited his father's lands and titles, serving King Henry III during campaigns in Wales and in Brittany. He died while returning from Brittany in 1230.

 WILLIAM D'ALBINI, LORD OF BELVOIR CASTLE

With estates that covered huge areas of the north and east midlands, including the family seat at Belvoir Castle (standing on a hilltop above the Vale of Belvoir in Leicestershire), Albini and his predecessors had been loyal servants of the Crown for generations.

Albini had supported King Richard I and Eleanor of Aquitaine against John when the king's brother had attempted to seize the throne while Richard was away on crusade. He even travelled to Germany to escort Richard back to England following his release from captivity.

When John eventually did become king, Albini served as Sheriff of Rutland, of Leicestershire, of Warwickshire and in a number of other roles that helped to bolster the administration of the realm. King John even appointed Albini to investigate irregularities in payments to the royal coffers in 1213, when he suspected the northern barons of plotting against him.

Being a loyal retainer, however, must also have given Albini a close and comprehensive view of the way that King John was running the country. This, as well as family ties and friendship with the rebel barons, may well have been what persuaded Albini to stand against the king on Magna Carta – although he did not join the rebel fold until after they had captured London in 1215. He was in command of Rochester Castle when King John laid siege to it in 1215, defending the castle bravely. When he followed common practice of sending the sick and wounded out of the castle, these posing no threat to the attackers, King John ordered that their hands and feet be hacked off.

The castle eventually fell to the king, and Albini was taken to Corfe castle in Dorset as a prisoner while King John headed for Belvoir, held by Albini's son, Nicholas. He forced the surrender of the castle by threatening Nicholas that he would starve Albini to death if he did not give in. Albini was ransomed for 6000 marks and freed when an initial instalment had been paid, although King John died before any further payments were made. When Albini swore allegiance to King Henry III, the remainder of the ransom was deferred to payments of just 40 marks a year.

Albini died in 1236, probably in his late seventies or eighties.

SIR EDWARD COKE

Known as the greatest lawyer of his generation, Sir Edward Coke was a great champion of Magna Carta, though he wasn't even born until more than 300 years after the charter was first issued by King John.

Coke is important in the Magna Carta story because of the way in which he refused to let the charter's ideals die. He promoted the right of individuals to be allowed a fair trial as well as their right not to be arrested or imprisoned without good reason, and believed that the power of the monarch to impose his (or her) will on the government and the legal system should be restricted.

Coke's support for Magna Carta and opposition to the actions of King Charles I in 1628 led to the English Parliament – in the House of Commons and the House of Lords – ratifying the Petition of Right. This was the first time that Parliament had united against the monarch on a major constitutional issue. Charles normally relied on his supporters in the House of Lords to keep the Commons under control, but with both houses siding against him, he had a major problem and the constitutional crisis eventually erupted into the English Civil War. The Petition of Right was to stand alongside Magna Carta and the later 1689 Bill of Rights as one of the most important constitutional documents in English history.

Yet, Coke was not an out-and-out rebel. During the course of his career, he served the Crown in a number of prestigious positions. Coke's father had been a barrister and was a wealthy man, able to send his son to a good school and to study at Cambridge University. Following in his father's footsteps, Coke became a lawyer and a successful barrister. In 1592, at the age of 40, he was appointed by Queen Elizabeth I as Solicitor General for England and Wales. He was also Attorney General under Queen Elizabeth and prosecuted several very high profile cases, including that of Robert Devereux, 2nd Earl of Essex, who was convicted of treason after leading a coup against the government. Devereux was the last person to be beheaded at the Tower of London.

Coke also prosecuted Sir Walter Raleigh – once a popular hero for his adventures as a soldier and as an explorer – for treason when he was accused of plotting to overthrow King James I. The evidence was flimsy, yet Coke secured a conviction and Raleigh, at first reprieved, was later executed. Coke was equally successful in prosecuting the eight main participants in the infamous Gunpowder Plot to blow up the Houses of Parliament.

While he was a zealous prosecutor when acting on behalf of the monarch, Coke actually believed wholeheartedly in the rule of law and in the way Magna Carta had prepared the way for everyone to enjoy the protection of the law. He was heavily involved as an investor in the development of England's new colonies in America, and was the man who drafted the Charter of Virginia in 1606, the document with which King James I granted exploitation rights to English settlers in the New World. The charter identified the land to be colonized and set out how taxes would be paid to the Crown but, crucially, Coke also included a clause ensuring that English subjects in America would enjoy the same rights under the law as anyone at home. The relevant paragraph reads:

> Also we do, for Us, our Heirs, and Successors, declare, by these Presents, that all and every the Persons being our Subjects, which shall dwell and inhabit within every or any of the said several Colonies and Plantations, and every of their children, which shall happen to be born within any of the Limits and Precincts of the said several Colonies and Plantations, shall have and enjoy all Liberties, Franchises, and Immunities, within any of our other Dominions, to all Intents and Purposes, as if they had been abiding and born, within this our Realm of England, or any other of our said Dominions.

This, along with Magna Carta, was used by the founding fathers to protest about their treatment by the British and to justify their rebellion, which led to the War of Independence 170 years later. Coke died in 1634 and is remembered for many achievements. Prime among these is his belief in a document – created 300 years before he was born – which led to his influencing events thousands of miles from England more than 140 years after he died.

 BOSTON

Originally named Trimountaine by the first English settlers to arrive in 1630 (referring to the three mountains that once dominated the peninsula), Boston was later officially named after the English town of Boston in Lincolnshire and became integral to the colonists' struggle for independence from Britain when they claimed their rights under Magna Carta.

By 1632, the city had become the capital of the English settlement known as the Massachusetts Bay Colony, and was well established as one of the most important harbours trading with the "Old World" in Europe, most specifically Britain.

Britain's American Customs Board had its headquarters in Boston from 1768, making the port a prime target for the activists who staged the "Boston Tea Party" in 1773. The demonstrators, disguised as dock workers and even Native Americans, boarded ships in the harbour that were carrying a huge consignment of tea. The tea belonged to the British East India Company and was part of a huge overstock that was being offloaded on the colonists, with the British Government also charging a new tax into the bargain. The entire shipment of tea was thrown overboard into the water.

The attack – in response to the new tea tax – was launched by a secret society called the Sons of Liberty. These political agitators included among their ranks John Adams, who would become the second President of the United States; his cousin Samuel Adams, who would become the Governor of Massachusetts; and the eventual turncoat Benedict Arnold.

The colonists in America had been suffering from a whole series of crippling taxes levied by the British Government, including the Stamp Act of 1765. This order basically demanded that printed materials in America, from legal documents, newspapers and magazines to humble playing cards, be produced only on paper that was imported from Britain and embossed with an official revenue stamp. As with the mounting toll of taxes levied on the British settlers in the American colonies, the duty had to paid using British currency rather than local money, making the tax even more of a burden on the fledgling economy.

The American colonists had no Members of Parliament to stand up for them in Westminster and demanded their rights under Magna Carta – the document states in Clause 12 that "No 'scutage' or 'aid' [tax] may be levied in our kingdom without its general consent..." While the taxes had been passed by parliament, the colonists were not represented there and therefore had not consented. They campaigned under the banner "No Taxation Without Representation" and the public demonstrations became increasingly disorderly.

Although France had been defeated by the British in the French and Indian War (which ended in 1763), the British were determined to station 10,000 troops permanently in America – a military presence that the colonists neither needed nor wanted. The troops were clearly intended as much to keep the colonists in line as they were for their protection.

The Boston Tea Party put the city at the centre of an escalating series of events, inspired by a claim to civil rights endowed by Magna Carta, that would lead to the American War of Independence two years later. The punitive action taken by the British also made it unfashionable and unpatriotic to drink tea in the colonies, leading to most Americans favouring coffee.

THOMAS JEFFERSON

A native of Virginia, Thomas Jefferson was born in April 1743 at his family home in Goochland County, now part of Albermarle County. He was one of 10 brothers and sisters. Although his family may have come from Wales originally, Jefferson was born and bred as an American. He came from a family of reasonably wealthy landowners and by the time he was 21, he would be running an extensive plantation.

Growing up, Jefferson was well educated and had a real thirst for knowledge. Displaying an avid intelligence, he learned to speak French, Greek, Italian, Latin and (eventually) Spanish. He studied architecture (designing several buildings in a classical style), mathematics, the sciences and philosophy, and graduated from The College of William and Mary in Williamsburg with honours in 1762.

It is reputed that Jefferson enjoyed studying for up to 15 hours a day and that he built up a library of more than 6,000 books over the course of his lifetime. Therefore, managing a plantation – as demanding as that was – could never be enough to hold the young man's interest. He became a lawyer and counted some of Virginia's elite amongst his clients, as well as some of its poorest people. Jefferson represented several slaves who were attempting to sue their masters for their freedom, and was known to speak out on issues of "personal liberty", although he owned a great many slaves himself.

Serving as a representative to the Second Continental Congress during the War of Independence, Jefferson became firm friends with one of the Congress leaders, John Adams, who pushed for Jefferson to draft the Declaration of Independence. Working with a few others on a small committee, Jefferson incorporated phrasing from a number of charters with which he was familiar, and made clear references to Sir Edward Coke's Petition of Right from 1628, the Bill of Rights from 1689 and, of course, Magna Carta, to use English law against the British Government.

Jefferson served as Governor of Virginia, and in 1784 he travelled to Europe as part of a delegation that included Benjamin Franklin and John Adams, to negotiate trade agreements with England, France and Spain. During the long journey across the Atlantic, he taught himself to read and write Spanish.

In Europe, Jefferson was able to indulge his passion for architecture in London, Paris and Madrid. While he was there, he took over from Franklin as United States Minister to France. Five years later, he became President George Washington's Secretary of State but resigned that role to pursue further political ambitions, being elected Vice President to John Adams in 1796 and the third President of the United States in 1800.

During two terms in office as president, Jefferson encouraged the push west to expand the territory of the United States before European nations could stake claims there. He brought Ohio into the union, bought Louisiana from the French and attempted to buy Florida from the Spanish. Expanding west led to the controversial resettlement of Native American peoples, but the mapping and exploration of the western continent was vital to the growth of the nation.

While his attitudes towards slavery and the Native Americans did not always sit well with the way that he championed liberty and the statement in the Declaration of Independence that "all men are created equal", Jefferson did play a vital role in creating the United States and set Magna Carta at the heart of the new nation.

PHILADELPHIA

Before the arrival of Europeans, the area that is now Philadelphia – the fifth-largest city in the United States – was populated by the Lenape Indians. When Dutch settlers arrived in the Delaware Valley in the early part of the seventeenth century, they built Fort Nassau and claimed the entire valley for the territory of New Netherland. When the Swedes arrived a few years later, they built Fort Christina and claimed their part of the valley as New Sweden.

The Dutch and Swedish colonists vied for control of the area until the Dutch eventually overcame the Swedes in 1655, only to be conquered themselves by the English in 1664. By 1681, King Charles II had granted William Penn a charter for the colony that was then named Pennsylvania, a combination of Penn's name and *silva* – the Latin word for forest land. Penn was an entrepreneur, the son of a prominent Royal Navy officer who, after the death of his father, had accepted the land in America as payment of a debt owed to Penn senior by the king.

Penn famously struck a bargain with the Lenape, buying the land in order that there would be peace between the Native Americans and the colonists. The city of Philadelphia (meaning "brotherly love" in Latin) grew out of Shackamaxon, the Lenape meeting place where Penn made the deal.

Over the next 20 years, Philadelphia grew into a major trading port and, due to the values of religious tolerance and good relations with the local Native Americans, settlers flocked to the area. By 1750, Philadelphia was a bigger and busier port than Boston, and had become second only to London in importance to the British Empire. One of its leading citizens,

Benjamin Franklin, worked to establish municipal services including one of America's first hospitals.

Philadelphia met Magna Carta head on when delegates from 12 of the 13 American colonies congregated there for the First Continental Congress in 1774, discussing their options for dealing with the colonists' grievances with King George III's government in Britain. They considered sanctions such as boycotting British goods, but events soon overtook them when the situation deteriorated into war a few months later.

The Second Continental Congress began in Philadelphia in the summer of 1775 and it was the following year, in the Assembly Room of Pennsylvania's administrative centre – now known as Independence Hall – that the Congress issued the Declaration of Independence on 4 July.

The main architect of the document, Thomas Jefferson, leant heavily on the English Bill of Rights from 1689, which had reiterated and extended some of the clauses of Magna Carta, and had pointed to Magna Carta itself.

The declaration accused King George of "imposing Taxes on us without our Consent", clearly contrary to Clause 12 of Magna Carta, and of "depriving us in many cases, of the benefit of Trial by Jury", which clearly stands against Clause 40: "To no one will we sell, to no one deny or delay right or justice."

However, Jefferson went way beyond Magna Carta or the Bill of Rights at the very beginning of the declaration where the preamble contained the famous lines:

"We hold these truths to be self-evident, that all men are created equal, that they are endowed by their Creator with certain unalienable Rights, that among these are Life, Liberty and the pursuit of Happiness."

The men gathered in the assembly room in Philadelphia were the leaders of their communities from all 13 colonies – the barons of America – and most had slaves whom they certainly did not regard as equal or endowed with any rights whatsoever. That issue, however, would be revisited when delegates met to sign the Constitution of the United States in Philadelphia 11 years later, although it would not be resolved for another century.

Philadelphia is one of the few cities in America that has played host to an original copy of Magna Carta. In 2007, Lincoln Cathedral's 1215 Magna Carta was sent on loan for exhibition at Philadelphia's National Constitution Center.

 # WASHINGTON DC

Nowhere is Magna Carta more revered than in the capital of the United States, Washington DC. Here, at the US National Archives, resides one of only two copies of Magna Carta that are held outside England. The Australian government owns one copy of the 1297 issue of Magna Carta, on display at Parliament House in Canberra, and American financier David Rubenstein presented the US copy – also the 1297 version – on permanent loan to the National Archives after purchasing it from the Perot Foundation for more than $20 million in 2007.

As well as the Rubenstein Magna Carta, there is another version of the document on display in Washington. In the eighteenth century, America's founding fathers saw Magna Carta as their blueprint for democratic government. It became fundamental to the Constitution of the United States, is still incorporated in full in the constitutions of more than a dozen US states and lies at the heart of government in America – quite literally.

At the eastern end of the National Mall stands one of the most famous structures in the world – the striking white dome of the United States Capitol, the seat of the US Congress. While the business of running the country is conducted in the main halls of the Capitol building, down in the crypt, underpinning the processes of government, stands a unique version of Magna Carta.

In a gold and white enamel display case there sits a panel with embossed gold lettering that duplicates the text of one of the 1215 copies of Magna Carta held in the British Library in London. Alongside the text are discs showing the front and back of King John's Great Seal, also rendered in gold. A representation of a medieval illustrated manuscript, using gold and precious stones, is in the other half of the case while standing between them is a glass panel etched in gold with an English translation of Magna Carta. The replica was created by English artist Louis Osman as a gift to the people of the United States from the people of Great Britain to celebrate the bicentenary of American independence in 1976.

Magna Carta also makes its presence felt in the US capital just a stone's throw to the east of the Capitol building at the Supreme Court. Although it looks like an ancient Greek temple transported from the Acropolis in Athens, the Supreme Court was actually only built in 1932. Behind the 16 marble columns that support the pediment above the main west entrance – which bears the legend "Equal Justice Under Law" – stand two massive bronze doors. Created by sculptor John Donnelly, the eight panels on the doors show historic scenes in the development of the law, the right-hand door decorated with scenes evocative of Magna Carta.

The scenes include Sir Edward Coke forbidding King James I to judge court cases, and King John sealing Magna Carta. The Magna Carta panel, bearing the words "Magna

Charta", shows John with a press used to emboss his seal into the customary mix of wax and resin, standing facing one of the barons, possibly "Marshal of the Army of God", Robert FitzWalter. Both men are armed with swords to demonstrate the tension, signifying that they are on the brink of conflict by standing with hands on their weapons. The king, however, shows that he has submitted to the will of the barons, as his sword is sheathed, hanging from his waist in its scabbard. FitzWalter's sword is in the open, the baron standing with both hands on the hilt – the tip of the sword rests on the ground at his feet, the hilt forming a cross as though he stands behind a large crucifix. This shows that he is ready to fight, but also that he stands in the right with God on his side. The panel can be interpreted with all of the aforementioned significance but it is, more than anything else, yet another indication of the great influence that Magna Carta has had on the laws and governance of the United States and the great esteem in which it is held in America, especially in Washington DC.

MAGNA CARTA, 1215: AN ESSENTIAL TRANSLATION

Magna Carta, as issued under the direction of King John and with his seal attached at the bottom, is not a very regal-looking document. In fact, although it would have looked a good deal less time worn when it was first produced 800 years ago, to our modern eyes it appears quite scrappy and untidy for such a serious legal document. Written on vellum using a quill pen, the words were an abbreviated form of medieval Latin, a kind of Latin shorthand. This has made the text difficult to interpret, even by Latin scholars and, as with so many legal documents, the actual meaning of certain sections has been contested over the years.

Anyone hoping to grasp the essence of the document, even someone who can decipher the Latin, is further hindered by the way that it runs on as continuous text, line after line, without any proper breaks. It wasn't until 1759 that England's first Professor of Law, William Blackstone, divided the document into the 63 clauses detailed below.

This translation is a version of the text that aims to outline the meaning of each clause rather than present a literal, word-for-word account. Based on the translation available from the British Library, there are additional notes in italics to highlight points of interest and to explain terms that, even in plain English, might be confusing for anyone not familiar with terminology relating to medieval feudalism.

THE CHARTER

JOHN, by the grace of God King of England, Lord of Ireland, Duke of Normandy and Aquitaine, and Count of Anjou, to his archbishops, bishops, abbots, earls, barons, justices, foresters, sheriffs, stewards, servants, and to all his officials and loyal subjects, Greeting.

[Magna Carta actually starts with a large drop-letter capital "I", the first letter of "Iohannes", or John.]

KNOW THAT BEFORE GOD, for the health of our soul and those of our ancestors and heirs, to the honour of God, the exaltation of the holy Church, and the better ordering of our kingdom, at the advice of our reverend fathers Stephen, Archbishop of Canterbury, Primate of all England, and Cardinal of the holy Roman Church; Henry, Archbishop of Dublin; William, Bishop of London; Peter, Bishop of Winchester; Jocelin, Bishop of Bath and Glastonbury; Hugh, Bishop of Lincoln; Walter, Bishop of Worcester; William, Bishop of Coventry; Benedict, Bishop of Rochester; Master Pandulf, subdeacon and member of the papal household; Brother Aymeric, Master of the Knighthood of the Temple in England; William Marshal, Earl of Pembroke; William, Earl of Salisbury; William, Earl of Warren; William, Earl of Arundel; Alan of Galloway, Constable of Scotland; Warin fitz Gerald; Peter fitz Herbert; Hubert de Burgh, Seneschal of Poitou; Hugh de Neville; Matthew fitz Herbert; Thomas Basset; Alan Basset; Philip Daubeny; Robert de Roppeley; John Marshal; John fitz Hugh, and other loyal subjects:

(Clause 1) FIRST, THAT WE HAVE GRANTED TO GOD, and by this present charter have confirmed for us and our heirs in perpetuity, that the English Church shall be free, and shall have its rights undiminished, and its liberties unimpaired. That we wish this so to be observed, appears from the fact that of our own free will, before the outbreak of the present dispute between us and our barons, we granted and confirmed by charter the freedom of the Church's elections – a right reckoned to be of the greatest necessity and importance to it – and caused this to be confirmed by Pope Innocent III. This freedom we shall observe ourselves, and desire to be observed in good faith by our heirs in perpetuity.

[Note the term "of our own free will", which was deliberately not used in later clauses in order to give King John the opportunity to complain to the Pope, when appealing for the document to be declared invalid, that the he was forced to agree to the terms under duress.]

TO ALL FREE MEN OF OUR KINGDOM we have also granted, for us and our heirs for ever, all the liberties written out below, to have and to keep for them and their heirs, of us and our heirs:

(Clause 2) If any earl, baron, or other person that holds lands directly of the Crown, for military service, shall die, and at his death his heir shall be of full age and owe a "relief", the heir shall have his inheritance on payment of the ancient scale of "relief". That is to say, the heir or heirs of an earl shall pay £100 for the entire earl's barony, the heir or heirs of a knight 100 shillings at most for the entire knight's "fee", and any man that owes less shall pay less, in accordance with the ancient usage of "fees".

[The "relief" is roughly equivalent to modern death duties or inheritance taxes. A knight's fee was an area of land granted to a knight, the land producing revenues sufficient for him to maintain himself in the manner required of a knight.]

(Clause 3) But if the heir of such a person is under age and a ward, when he comes of age he shall have his inheritance without "relief" or fine.

(Clause 4) The guardian of the land of an heir who is under age shall take from it only reasonable revenues, customary dues, and feudal services. He shall do this without destruction or damage to men or property. If we have given the guardianship of the land to a sheriff, or to any person answerable to us for the revenues, and he commits destruction or damage, we will exact compensation from him, and the land shall be entrusted to two worthy and prudent men of the same "fee", who shall be answerable to us for the revenues, or to the person to whom we have assigned them. If we have given or sold to anyone the guardianship of such land, and he causes destruction or damage, he shall lose the guardianship of it, and it shall be handed over to two worthy and prudent men of the same "fee", who shall be similarly answerable to us.

(Clause 5) For so long as a guardian has guardianship of such land, he shall maintain the houses, parks, fish preserves, ponds, mills, and everything else pertaining to it, from the revenues of the land itself. When the heir comes of age, he shall restore the whole land to him, stocked with plough teams and such implements of husbandry as the season demands and the revenues from the land can reasonably bear.

(Clause 6) Heirs may be given in marriage, but not to someone of lower social standing. Before a marriage takes place, it shall be made known to the heir's next-of-kin.

(Clause 7) At her husband's death, a widow may have her marriage portion and inheritance at once and without trouble. She shall pay nothing for her dower, marriage portion, or any inheritance that she and her husband held jointly on the day of his death. She may remain in her husband's house for forty days after his death, and within this period her dower shall be assigned to her.

[A "dower" was a sum of money or property that a husband pledged to his wife at the time of their marriage, something on which she could rely should he die before she did. This is not to be confused with a dowry, which was a sum of money or property given by the bride's parents to the groom or his family.]

(Clause 8) No widow shall be compelled to marry, so long as she wishes to remain without a husband. But if she holds lands from the Crown, she must give security that she will not marry without royal consent, or without the consent of whatever other lord from whom she may hold lands.

(Clause 9) Neither we nor our officials will seize any land or rent in payment of a debt, so long as the debtor has movable goods sufficient to discharge the debt. A debtor's sureties shall not be distrained upon so long as the debtor himself can discharge his debt. If, for lack of means, the debtor is unable to discharge his debt, his sureties shall be answerable for it. If they so desire, they may have the debtor's lands and rents until they have received satisfaction for the debt that they

paid for him, unless the debtor can show that he has settled his obligations to them.

[Sureties were, and still are, people who guarantee to take responsibility for a borrower's debts should the borrower be unable to repay.]

(Clause 10) If anyone who has borrowed a sum of money from Jews dies before the debt has been repaid, his heir shall pay no interest on the debt for so long as he remains under age, irrespective of from whom he holds his lands. If such a debt falls into the hands of the Crown, it will take nothing except the principal sum specified in the bond.

[At the time when the Magna Carta was drafted, Christians were banned from lending money on which interest could be charged, specific verses in the Old Testament having forbidden it:

Deuteronomy 23:19–20: "You shall not charge interest on loans to your brother, interest on money, interest on food, interest on anything that is lent for interest. You may charge a foreigner interest, but you may not charge your brother interest ..."

The same rules applied to Jews (and also applies in Islam), but they interpreted the scriptures differently, allowing themselves to lend money to those who weren't Jewish. In this way, the Jewish community became widely involved in moneylending.]

(Clause 11) If a man dies owing money to Jews, his wife may have her dower and pay nothing towards the debt from it. If he leaves children that are under age, their needs may also be

provided for on a scale appropriate to the size of his holding of lands. The debt is to be paid out of the residue, reserving the service due to his feudal lords. Debts owed to persons other than Jews are to be dealt with similarly.

(Clause 12) No "scutage" or "aid" may be levied in our kingdom without its general consent, unless it is for the ransom of our person, to make our eldest son a knight, and (once) to marry our eldest daughter. For these purposes only a reasonable "aid" may be levied. "Aids" from the city of London are to be treated similarly.

["Scutage" was the name of the cash alternative that a knight or other nobleman expected to do military service could pay in order to avoid going to war. "Aid" in this instance simply means "tax".]

(Clause 13) The city of London shall enjoy all its ancient liberties and free customs, both by land and by water. We also will and grant that all other cities, boroughs, towns, and ports shall enjoy all their liberties and free customs.

(Clause 14) To obtain the general consent of the realm for the assessment of an "aid" – except in the three cases specified above – or a "scutage", we will cause the archbishops, bishops, abbots, earls, and greater barons to be summoned individually by letter. To those who hold lands directly of us we will cause a general summons to be issued, through the sheriffs and other officials, to come together on a fixed day (of which at least forty days notice shall be given) and at a fixed place. In all letters of summons, the cause of the summons will be stated. When a summons has been issued, the business appointed for the day shall go forward in accordance with the resolution of those present, even if not all those who were summoned have appeared.

(Clause 15) In future we will allow no one to levy an "aid" from his free men, except to ransom his person, to make his eldest son a knight, and (once) to marry his eldest daughter. For these purposes only a reasonable "aid" may be levied.

(Clause 16) No man shall be forced to perform more service for a knight's "fee", or other free holding of land, than is due from it.

(Clause 17) Ordinary lawsuits shall not follow the royal court around, but shall be held in a fixed place.

(Clause 18) Inquests of novel disseisin, mort d'ancestor, and darrein presentment shall be taken only in their proper county court. We ourselves, or in our absence abroad our chief justice, will send two justices to each county four times a year, and these justices, with four knights of the county elected by the county itself, shall hold the assizes in the county court, on the day and in the place where the court meets.

[An "inquest of novel disseisin" was a hearing dealing with someone who was taking action to recover land that had recently been taken from him, land of which he had been newly [novel] dispossessed or disseised. "Mort d'ancestor" dealt with property disputes following the death of a relative, and "darrein presentment" was related to landowners' disputes over the responsibility for the appointment of local clergymen.]

(Clause 19) If any assizes cannot be taken on the day of the county court, as many knights and freeholders shall afterwards remain behind, of those who have attended the

court, as will suffice for the administration of justice, having regard to the volume of business to be done.

(Clause 20) For a trivial offence, a free man shall be fined only in proportion to the degree of his offence, and for a serious offence correspondingly, but not so heavily as to deprive him of his livelihood. In the same way, a merchant shall be spared his merchandise, and a villein the implements of his husbandry, if they fall upon the mercy of a royal court. None of these fines shall be imposed except by the assessment on oath of reputable men of the neighbourhood.

[A villein, sometimes spelled villain, was not a crook, but a type of serf who was just one rung of the ladder above the lowliest of peasants.]

(Clause 21) Earls and barons shall be fined only by their equals, and in proportion to the gravity of their offence.

(Clause 22) A fine imposed upon the lay property of a clerk in holy orders shall be assessed upon the same principles, without reference to the value of his ecclesiastical benefice.

[Clergymen of all ranks could receive a "benefice" from the church or from a local benefactor as a payment for their services or a retainer for future services.]

(Clause 23) No town or person shall be forced to build bridges over rivers except those with an ancient obligation to do so.

(Clause 24) No sheriff, constable, coroners, or other royal officials are to hold lawsuits that should be held by the royal justices.

(Clause 25) Every county, hundred, wapentake, and tithing shall remain at its ancient rent, without increase, except the royal demesne manors.

[The terms "hundred, wapentake, and tithing" refer to different ways that small administrative areas within a county might be termed. The royal demesne manors were properties and land held by the crown that had not been granted or let to anyone else.]

(Clause 26) If at the death of a man who holds a lay "fee" of the Crown, a sheriff or royal official produces royal letters patent of summons for a debt due to the Crown, it shall be lawful for them to seize and list movable goods found in the lay "fee" of the dead man to the value of the debt, as assessed by worthy men. Nothing shall be removed until the whole debt is paid, when the residue shall be given over to the executors to carry out the dead man's will. If no debt is due to the Crown, all the movable goods shall be regarded as the property of the dead man, except the reasonable shares of his wife and children.

(Clause 27) If a free man dies intestate, his movable goods are to be distributed by his next-of-kin and friends, under the supervision of the Church. The rights of his debtors are to be preserved.

(Clause 28) No constable or other royal official shall take corn or other movable goods from any man without immediate payment, unless the seller voluntarily offers postponement of this.

(Clause 29) No constable may compel a knight to pay money for castle-guard if the knight is willing to undertake the guard

in person, or with reasonable excuse to supply some other fit man to do it. A knight taken or sent on military service shall be excused from castle-guard for the period of this service.

[Castle-guard, literally mounting guard on a royal castle or the castle of his overlord, was one of the military obligations a knight was expected to undertake under the feudal system.]

(Clause 30) No sheriff, royal official, or other person shall take horses or carts for transport from any free man, without his consent.

(Clause 31) Neither we nor any royal official will take wood for our castle, or for any other purpose, without the consent of the owner.

(Clause 32) We will not keep the lands of people convicted of felony in our hand for longer than a year and a day, after which they shall be returned to the lords of the "fees" concerned.

(Clause 33) All fish-weirs shall be removed from the Thames, the Medway, and throughout the whole of England, except on the sea coast.

[Fish-weirs were used for trapping fish but prevented migration and were a threat in the long term to the survival of fish stocks in the rivers.]

(Clause 34) The writ called precipe shall not in future be issued to anyone in respect of any holding of land, if a free man could thereby be deprived of the right of trial in his own lord's court.

[The "writ of precipe" was a command issued by the king directing legal officers to take action against someone.]

(Clause 35) There shall be standard measures of wine, ale, and corn (the London quarter), throughout the kingdom. There shall also be a standard width of dyed cloth, russet, and haberject, namely two ells within the selvedges. Weights are to be standardised similarly.

[Haberject was cloth of mixed colours, an ell was a unit of measurement equal to about 45 inches (1.14m) and selvedges were the edges of the cloth where the weave was finished off to stop it unravelling.]

(Clause 36) In future nothing shall be paid or accepted for the issue of a writ of inquisition from him that desires an inquisition of life or limbs. It shall be given gratis, and not refused.

[A "writ of inquisition" was a document sent to a sheriff or other legal official instructing him to investigate whether a person held for a crime such as murder had been fairly accused. This clause helped to ensure that accused persons received a fair trial.]

(Clause 37) If a man holds land of the Crown by "fee-farm", "socage", or "burgage", and also holds land of someone else for knight's service, we will not have guardianship of his heir, nor of the land that belongs to the other person's "fee", by virtue of the "fee-farm", "socage", or "burgage", unless the "fee-farm" owes knight's service. We will not have the guardianship of a man's heir, or of land that he holds of someone else, by reason of any small property that he may hold of the Crown for a service of knives, arrows, or the like.

*["Fee-farm", "socage", and "burgage" refer to different
kinds of rent or feudal obligation due from tenants.
Burgage was usually associated with properties in towns or
"boroughs".]*

(Clause 38) In future no official shall place a man on trial
upon his own unsupported statement, without producing
credible witnesses to the truth of it.

(Clause 39) No free man shall be seized or imprisoned, or
stripped of his rights or possessions, or outlawed or exiled,
or deprived of his standing in any way, nor will we proceed
with force against him, or send others to do so, except by the
lawful judgment of his equals or by the law of the land.

(Clause 40) To no one will we sell, to no one deny or delay
right or justice.

(Clause 41) All merchants may enter or leave England
unharmed and without fear, and may stay or travel within it,
by land or water, for purposes of trade, free from all illegal
exactions, in accordance with ancient and lawful customs.
This, however, does not apply in time of war to merchants
from a country that is at war with us. Any such merchants
found in our country at the outbreak of war shall be detained
without injury to their persons or property, until we or
our chief justice have discovered how our own merchants
are being treated in the country at war with us. If our own
merchants are safe they shall be safe too.

(Clause 42) In future it shall be lawful for any man to leave
and return to our kingdom unharmed and without fear, by
land or water, preserving his allegiance to us, except in time
of war, for some short period, for the common benefit of

the realm. People that have been imprisoned or outlawed in accordance with the law of the land, people from a country that is at war with us, and merchants – who shall be dealt with as stated above – are excepted from this provision.

(Clause 43) If a man holds lands of any "escheat" such as the "honour" of Wallingford, Nottingham, Boulogne, Lancaster, or of other "escheats" in our hand that are baronies, at his death his heir shall give us only the "relief" and service that he would have made to the baron, had the barony been in the baron's hand. We will hold the "escheat" in the same manner as the baron held it.

(Clause 44) People who live outside the forest need not in future appear before the royal justices of the forest in answer to general summonses, unless they are actually involved in proceedings or are sureties for someone who has been seized for a forest offence.

(Clause 45) We will appoint as justices, constables, sheriffs, or other officials, only men that know the law of the realm and are minded to keep it well.

(Clause 46) All barons who have founded abbeys, and have charters of English kings or ancient tenure as evidence of this, may have guardianship of them when there is no abbot, as is their due.

(Clause 47) All forests that have been created in our reign shall at once be disafforested. River-banks that have been enclosed in our reign shall be treated similarly.

(Clause 48) All evil customs relating to forests and warrens, foresters, warreners, sheriffs and their servants, or river-

banks and their wardens, are at once to be investigated in every county by twelve sworn knights of the county, and within forty days of their enquiry the evil customs are to be abolished completely and irrevocably. But we, or our chief justice if we are not in England, are first to be informed.

(Clause 49) We will at once return all hostages and charters delivered up to us by Englishmen as security for peace or for loyal service.

(Clause 50) We will remove completely from their offices the kinsmen of Gerard de Athée, and in future they shall hold no offices in England. The people in question are Engelard de Cigogné, Peter, Guy, and Andrew de Chanceaux, Guy de Cigogné, Geoffrey de Martigny and his brothers, Philip Marc and his brothers, with Geoffrey his nephew, and all their followers.

(Clause 51) As soon as peace is restored, we will remove from the kingdom all the foreign knights, bowmen, their attendants, and the mercenaries that have come to it, to its harm, with horses and arms.

(Clause 52) To any man whom we have deprived or dispossessed of lands, castles, liberties, or rights, without the lawful judgment of his equals, we will at once restore these. In cases of dispute the matter shall be resolved by the judgment of the twenty-five barons referred to below in the clause for securing the peace *(see Clause 61)*. In cases, however, where a man was deprived or dispossessed of something without the lawful judgment of his equals by our father King Henry or our brother King Richard, and it remains in our hands or is held by others under our warranty, we shall have respite for the period commonly allowed to Crusaders, unless a lawsuit

had been begun, or an enquiry had been made at our order, before we took the Cross as a Crusader. On our return from the Crusade, or if we abandon it, we will at once render justice in full.

*(Clause 53)*We shall have similar respite in rendering justice in connexion with forests that are to be disafforested, or to remain forests, when these were first afforested by our father Henry or our brother Richard; with the guardianship of lands in another person's "fee", when we have hitherto had this by virtue of a "fee" held of us for knight's service by a third party; and with abbeys founded in another person's "fee", in which the lord of the "fee" claims to own a right. On our return from the Crusade, or if we abandon it, we will at once do full justice to complaints about these matters.

(Clause 54) No one shall be arrested or imprisoned on the appeal of a woman for the death of any person except her husband.

(Clause 55) All fines that have been given to us unjustly and against the law of the land, and all fines that we have exacted unjustly, shall be entirely remitted or the matter decided by a majority judgment of the twenty-five barons referred to below in the clause for securing the peace (*see Clause 61*) together with Stephen, archbishop of Canterbury, if he can be present, and such others as he wishes to bring with him. If the archbishop cannot be present, proceedings shall continue without him, provided that if any of the twenty-five barons has been involved in a similar suit himself, his judgment shall be set aside, and someone else chosen and sworn in his place, as a substitute for the single occasion, by the rest of the twenty-five.

(Clause 56) If we have deprived or dispossessed any Welshmen of land, liberties, or anything else in England or in Wales, without the lawful judgment of their equals, these are at once to be returned to them. A dispute on this point shall be determined in the Marches by the judgment of equals. English law shall apply to holdings of land in England, Welsh law to those in Wales, and the law of the Marches to those in the Marches. The Welsh shall treat us and ours in the same way.

(Clause 57) In cases where a Welshman was deprived or dispossessed of anything, without the lawful judgment of his equals, by our father King Henry or our brother King Richard, and it remains in our hands or is held by others under our warranty, we shall have respite for the period commonly allowed to Crusaders, unless a lawsuit had been begun, or an enquiry had been made at our order, before we took the Cross as a Crusader. But on our return from the Crusade, or if we abandon it, we will at once do full justice according to the laws of Wales and the said regions.

(Clause 58) We will at once return the son of Llywelyn, all Welsh hostages, and the charters delivered to us as security for the peace.

(Clause 59) With regard to the return of the sisters and hostages of Alexander, King of Scotland, his liberties and his rights, we will treat him in the same way as our other barons of England, unless it appears from the charters that we hold from his father William, formerly king of Scotland, that he should be treated otherwise. This matter shall be resolved by the judgment of his equals in our court.

(Clause 60) All these customs and liberties that we have granted shall be observed in our kingdom in so far as

concerns our own relations with our subjects. Let all men of our kingdom, whether clergy or laymen, observe them similarly in their relations with their own men.

(Clause 61) SINCE WE HAVE GRANTED ALL THESE THINGS for God, for the better ordering of our kingdom, and to allay the discord that has arisen between us and our barons, and since we desire that they shall be enjoyed in their entirety, with lasting strength, for ever, we give and grant to the barons the following security:

The barons shall elect twenty-five of their number to keep, and cause to be observed with all their might, the peace and liberties granted and confirmed to them by this charter.

If we, our chief justice, our officials, or any of our servants offend in any respect against any man, or transgress any of the articles of the peace or of this security, and the offence is made known to four of the said twenty-five barons, they shall come to us – or in our absence from the kingdom to the chief justice – to declare it and claim immediate redress. If we, or in our absence abroad the chief justice, make no redress within forty days, reckoning from the day on which the offence was declared to us or to him, the four barons shall refer the matter to the rest of the twenty-five barons, who may distrain upon and assail us in every way possible, with the support of the whole community of the land, by seizing our castles, lands, possessions, or anything else saving only our own person and those of the queen and our children, until they have secured such redress as they have determined upon. Having secured the redress, they may then resume their normal obedience to us.

Any man who so desires may take an oath to obey the commands of the twenty-five barons for the achievement of these ends, and to join with them in assailing us to the utmost of his power. We give public and free permission to take this oath to any man who so desires, and at no time will we prohibit any man from taking it. Indeed, we will compel any of our subjects who are unwilling to take it to swear it at our command.

If one of the twenty-five barons dies or leaves the country, or is prevented in any other way from discharging his duties, the rest of them shall choose another baron in his place, at their discretion, who shall be duly sworn in as they were.

In the event of disagreement among the twenty-five barons on any matter referred to them for decision, the verdict of the majority present shall have the same validity as a unanimous verdict of the whole twenty-five, whether these were all present or some of those summoned were unwilling or unable to appear.

The twenty-five barons shall swear to obey all the above articles faithfully, and shall cause them to be obeyed by others to the best of their power.

We will not seek to procure from anyone, either by our own efforts or those of a third party, anything by which any part of these concessions or liberties might be revoked or diminished. Should such a thing be procured, it shall be null and void and we will at no time make use of it, either ourselves or through a third party.

(Clause 62) We have remitted and pardoned fully to all men any ill-will, hurt, or grudges that have arisen between us and our subjects, whether clergy or laymen, since the beginning of the dispute. We have in addition remitted fully, and for our own part have also pardoned, to all clergy and laymen any

offences committed as a result of the said dispute between Easter in the sixteenth year of our reign (i.e. 1215) and the restoration of peace.

In addition we have caused letters patent to be made for the barons, bearing witness to this security and to the concessions set out above, over the seals of Stephen archbishop of Canterbury, Henry archbishop of Dublin, the other bishops named above, and Master Pandulf.

(Clause 63) IT IS ACCORDINGLY OUR WISH AND COMMAND that the English Church shall be free, and that men in our kingdom shall have and keep all these liberties, rights, and concessions, well and peaceably in their fullness and entirety for them and their heirs, of us and our heirs, in all things and all places for ever.

Both we and the barons have sworn that all this shall be observed in good faith and without deceit. Witness the abovementioned people and many others.

Given by our hand in the meadow that is called Runnymede, between Windsor and Staines, on the fifteenth day of June in the seventeenth year of our reign.

FURTHER READING

Numerous books have been written about life in the middle ages, Magna Carta, the Plantagenet dynasty and the many fascinating people of this era. Here are a few suggestions for further reading.

British History Encyclopedia (Paragon, 1999)

Gravett, Christopher, Eyewitness Guides: Knight (Dorling Kinderskey, 1993) and Eyewitness Guides: Castles (Dorling Kindersley, 1994)

Kenyon, Sherrilyn, *Everyday Life in the Middle Ages* (Writer's Digest Books, 1995)

Kramer, Ann, Eleanor of Aquitaine (National Geographic, 2006)

Macdonald, Fiona, A Medieval Castle (Peter Bedrick Books, 1990)

Weir, Alison, Britain's Royal Families: The Complete Genealogy (Pimlico, 2002)

Whittock, Martyn, A Brief History of Life in the Middle Ages (Robinson, 2009)

The following institutions and web resources provide useful and interesting information surrounding the history of Magna Carta:

The translation of the full text of Magna Carta, reproduced on pages 137–156, is taken from the British Library: www.bl.uk/magna-carta/articles/magna-carta-english-translation

Magna Carta 800th Anniversary website:
www.magnacarta800th.com

Library of Congress: www.loc.gov

Supreme Court of the United States: www.supremecourt.gov

National Park Service: www.nps.gov

Architect of the Capitol: www.aoc.gov

The Official Website of the British Monarchy:
www.royal.gov.uk

Royal Collection Trust: www.royalcollection.org.uk

Museum of London: www.museumoflondon.org.uk

The National Trust: www.nationaltrust.org.uk

The History of England: www.england-history.org

History Today: www.historytoday.com

OTHER TITLES IN THIS SERIES INCLUDE:

THE TUDOR TREASURY
A collection of fascinating facts and insights about the Tudor dynasty
Elizabeth Norton

ISBN: 9780233004334

THE AGINCOURT COMPANION
A guide to the legendary battle and warfare in the medieval world
Anne Curry

ISBN: 9780233004716

A VICTORIAN TREASURY
A collection of fascinating facts and insights about the Victorian era
Lucinda Hawksley

ISBN: 9780233004778